# Honoring Work and Life

## 99 Words for Leaders to Live By

Dr. Joseph Koob

Copyright © 2008 by Dr. Joseph Koob

ISBN  0-7414-4824-6


First Edition

A difficultpeople.org publication

Published by:

PUBLISHING.COM

1094 New DeHaven Street, Suite 100
West Conshohocken, PA 19428-2713
Info@buybooksontheweb.com
www.buybooksontheweb.com
Toll-free  (877) BUY BOOK
Local Phone (610) 941-9999
Fax  (610) 941-9959

Printed in the United States of America

Printed on Recycled Paper

Published  June 2008

# 99 Words for Leaders to Live By

**INTEGRITY**

1. Integrity
2. Honesty**
3. Trust
4. Ownership
5. Accountable
6. Responsibility
7. Reliability
8. Self-control**
9. Loyalty
10. Committed
11. Conscientious
12. Credible
13. Stability
14. Continuity
15. Disciplined
16. Humility
17. Idealism

**SERVICE** to Others

18. Service
19. Appreciation
20. Acknowledgment
21. Respect
22. Courteous
23. Attention
24. Support
25. Grateful (Thanking People)
26. Recognition
27. Celebration
28. Ceremony
29. Reward

**HONORING** the Humanity of Others

30. Caring
31. Kindness**
32. Empathy
33. Compassion
34. Patience
35. Generous
36. Responsiveness
37. Grace

**PERCEPTION**

38. Self-awareness**
39. Awareness
40. Visibility
41. Connecting
42. Modeling

**SELF-VALUE**

43. Self-worth**
44. Self-respect
45. Self-confidence**
46. Character
47. Identity

**QUALITY**

48. Quality
49. Value-added
50. Stretching
51. Learning
52. Education
53. Renewal
54. Solution-focused
55. Catalyst
56. Cultivate
57. Rigorous

**PERSONAL APPROACH**

58. Persistence
59. Synthesizer
60. Cohesion
61. Attitude
62. Consistent
63. Cooperative
64. Competent
65. Discerning

66. Focus
67. Organized
68. Engagement
69. Determined
70. Energy
71. Down-to-earth
72. Simplicity

**FREE YOURSELF**

73. Creativity
74. Innovation
75. Flexibility
76. Experiment
77. Risk-taking
78. Fluidity
79. Chances
80. Imagination
81. Friction-free
82. Anticipates
83. Facilitates
84. Curiosity
85. Initiative
86. Choices

**LIVE LIFE OUT LOUD**

87. Passion

88. Vision

89. Conviction

90. Courage

91. Fearless

92. Zany

93. Spontaneous

94. Zesty

95. Intensity

96. Charisma

97. Showmanship

98. Positivity**

99. Symbolizes


**The Seven Keys to Understanding and Working with Difficult People

# PREFACE

This book is the second of three works inspired by members of difficultpeople.org.* The first of this series *Difficult Situations: Dealing with Change*, was researched and written during a time of significant change in my life and in the lives of some of our members. This book and penultimate book of this Trilogy, *Leaders Managing Change,* address the more specific issues of how to best deal with Change in today's business environment.

While this book can stand on its own merits, it also serves as a introduction to *Leaders Managing Change*. The essential purpose is to provide a foundation of key ideas through focusing on Leadership and Personal qualities, attributes, and behaviors that honor not only our work but our life. It is my firm belief that true leaders work to serve their fellow employees, their team, their company, their customers, as well as their families and friends.

## Why 99?

The terms chosen for inclusion in this work are drawn from a wide range of sources as well as personal experience as a leader/ manager, coach, counselor, mentor, educator, and human being. In researching this book I have read many works that espouse excellent concepts for leadership and for working successfully through change. Time and again key ideas were brought out by disparate authors using the same or very similar terminology.

After compiling a long list of key ideas from all of these sources, as well as drawing from my own experience and writings, I organized these key words into categories reflective of what I felt were key leadership skills. Then I began to narrow the list down into what I consider to be the most significant, all-encompassing ideas for the business leader.

*Change Trilogy: *Dealing with Change*: Difficult Situations: Dealing with Change; Honoring Work and Life: 99 Words for Leaders to Live By; Leaders Managing Change,*

As I focused on what I considered to be the most important concepts to discuss, the list narrowed and subsequently I adjusted it to cover the ideas I felt were most important. Some terms were deleted in favor of similar terms where I felt the 'winner' said it better. Sometimes I kept terms that seem very much alike, but also have slight, but important changes in perspective. Ultimately when I was close to 100 terms I settled on '99' because '100' just seemed too perfect and too convenient, AND 99 seemed much 'Zestier' (see #94).

Specific words were chosen for their impact. Thus I did not aim to choose terms that fit conveniently together – like all nouns, or all adjectives. If a word struck me as somewhat more insightful or zesty in one form than another, that is how I made the selection. You may find other terms or word forms that fit your personality and style better than my choices do. This list is by no means exhaustive and I encourage you to find your truth by jotting notes in the margin and adding to what is here.

## What makes this book different?

There are many books out there on Leadership and Change. Why does the business world need two more? How will these two works add value to an already crowded field?

I feel that my unique value as an author is that I can bring a wide body of ideas together and condense them into a fundamental, down-to-earth, easily accessible form. As a long-time educator I determined long ago that students (of any type and age) will not read something thoroughly unless they can get through it readily. And what they don't read, they don't 'get.'

Thus, in essence, this is a meta-study of the different types of leadership materials out there, aimed at bringing a wide range of ideas into two succinct works.

One might ask the question, "What qualities, what values, what ideas make a leader great? And my answer to that would be, "The value and qualities that are closest to that person's heart, as well as the personal dedication and power to bring those to the fore when working with people."

## The Sources

In preparing for writing about Leadership and Change I gathered a cross-section of materials from the 'Change' literature and the 'Leadership/Business Change' literature. There are many excellent works available and I let the author of one work lead me to others. Other books just serendipitously landed in my lap in one way or another.

My technique is to read an entire book, highlight it as I go, type up my notes from the book, and then rearrange those notes just before I start to write. So while my experience plays a major role in what and how I write about Change and Leadership, I also owe a debt to the works contained in the bibliography. All of these books have had useful ideas and materials and I recommend that the serious student of Quality Leadership read as much as possible.

I would particularly like to point out the invaluable ideas found in Thomas Peters' books (my personal favorite is *The Pursuit of Wow*); and John Maxwell's and William Bridges' works.

## Words, Words, Words

The key ideas presented in this book come from many sources as well as personal experience. Therefore, in most cases it is impossible to give individual credit for any value or quality discussed to one specific author. However, if I feel an author has provided inspiration to my selecting 'their' word, I will indicate that throughout this text. Quotes and paraphrases from authors' works are acknowledged.

## Leaders Managing Change

Following on the heels of this book will be the creation of the book *Leaders Managing Change*. This work focuses on bringing the knowledge, skills, and tools that middle managers need to be successful in the constantly changing business climate today.

## Thanks to...

All the authors and works in the bibliography. I admire your work and contributions to this arena.

Heath Potter, design specialist and web-master, for all your hard work in your hectic schedule.

My readers: Anne, Lisa, Nathan, and Steve.

Life and its funny way of telling me what I need to do next.

# INTRODUCTION

My emphasis is writing books that I sincerely hope are of use to business leaders today. These works focus on "Understanding and Working through Difficult Situations." My style is to write in a format that is easy-to-read, educational, and that allows the reader the opportunity to build his/her knowledge from chapter to chapter. I bring to the table many years as a college educator, executive and business coach, counselor, and manager. I have done and continue to do extensive research and reading in the business literature and feel that my works present a comprehensive approach to business concerns today. [See the annotated bibliography of my works in Appendix IV, specifically "Books with a Business Focus"]

## The Order of Things

The grouping of terms under selected headings is a personal choice based on how I feel these ideas relate to each other and to our roles as leaders. There is, however, method to my madness in formatting the main sections and the order of word presentation. Many of the terms are interrelated and I have tried to set-up a flow from one section and one word to another.

The organization of the major sections is also purposeful. I have chosen to start with what I feel are terms that set a foundation for who we are as leaders and human beings, followed very closely by the importance of terms that formulate who we are in our interactions with others. These two sections then meld into more down-to-earth personal qualities, and the final two sections build from there and focus on our approach to work and life.

Individual term placement was also a prime consideration. Flow and relational ideas between adjacent terms was paramount. Beginning and ending terms have a special significance to the category and to me, personally. Finally there are seven starred (**) terms in the "Contents" list and high-lighted in the text. These are "The Seven Keys to Being Successful with Difficult People" as delineated in the various books produced for difficultpeople.org.

Dr. Joseph Koob

## Choices

How one reads a text is certainly personal. However as a broad recommendation, since each term will have its own chapter or section, the reader might find it useful to read one, or several, item(s) per day, allowing time to reflect on the significance and importance of that concept in their own work, life, and managerial/leadership style.

Another technique might be to read the entire work and then return to those items that seem to be of particular interest, choosing then to re-focus on certain choices on a daily or weekly basis for personal development.

One particularly valuable approach would be to take all the terms and rate them according to your strengths and weaknesses in your own leadership style. Then use this knowledge to pay closer attention to how you use your strengths within your daily/weekly work routine and how you can develop those areas you feel you have a need to improve. [See Appendices I and II for two scales you can use for this purpose.]

Some of these terms you will probably find are very significant to how you approach your work and life. Others may not seem as critical or as motivating and you probably will have a different perspective that works better for you.

I have selected terms that have been important to me through my experiences in my work and in my life and terms that have been highlighted by other authors that I feel are of major significance. Semantics can, however, play a major role in how we look at things. For instance, I may use an adverbial/adjectival form of a word because that has the most meaning for me, however, you may feel a verb or noun has more significance for you.

In selecting the words and the form of any given word (noun, verb, adjective, etc.), I chose what I felt had the most meaning and impact. I also use a variety of other terms that didn't make the top 99 throughout the text to help delineate the main concepts further. You may find some of these other words and phrases are worth making note of because they have a stronger association for you. This is one of those books that is meant to be 'marked up.' Your best learning will come from manipulating these materials in whatever ways help you grow the most as a manager and leader.

I am a person who takes words and ideas and puts them on my refrigerator, in my wallet, and tape them to my computer so I have a reminder of what I think is important, what to focus on, and what I feel I need to work on in my own life and work. Whatever works for you!

Our goal is to provide you with thought-provoking material that will help you become a stronger and more capable, kinder leader for your team and organization. We hope it will also help you enjoy your work and life to the utmost.

Sincerely,

Joe Koob

# PART I
# INTEGRITY

## 1. Integrity

Synonyms: uprightness; honor; moral soundness; sincerity; reliable

Antonyms: dishonor; disgrace; unreliable; dishonest

In-te-gri-ty: 1. The quality or state of being complete; unbroken condition; wholeness; entirety 2. The quality or state of being unimpaired; perfect condition; soundness 3. The quality or state of being of sound moral principle; uprightness, honesty, and sincerity – SYN. See Honesty

(Webster's New World Dictionary)

When we think of integrity we can conjure up a wide variety of concepts and images that help us to narrow the field. However, actually putting our finger on what defines the quality of integrity is, I feel, much more difficult than a definition provided by a dictionary. We might easily identify a person who we admire by saying, "She has integrity," but what do we really mean?

Integrity is a feeling, a quality, more than a definable fact. And as such, I believe that as leaders we need to consider some very important perspectives relevant to this quality:

> How we perceive ourselves – do we truly feel we are 'in integrity?' (Perkins)

> How do we come across to others – do they feel we are 'in integrity' in our dealings, interactions, and work with them?

How do we perceive integrity in others – do we respect this quality in the people we come in contact with throughout our day?

Each of these perspectives is critical to who we are as a leader.

## In Integrity

(Betty Perkins, *Lion Taming*)

My readers and I have tossed this phraseology back and forth a good bit. I really like the action-oriented perspective of being 'in integrity.' However, some of my readers really don't like this phrasing and like 'integrous' better or simply, 'having integrity.' Of course, I could just rewrite the whole book using just 'integrity' and changing the sentence structure, but then that wouldn't be very **Creative** (See Chapter 73) or **Zesty** (See Chapter 94).

### Are you 'In Integrity'

I believe we all want to be honorable people. Even when life is difficult and we have tough choices to make, most of us wish to maintain a high-quality image of who we are and what we are about. Taking the time to consider this in some depth is an excellent exercise, particularly if we are dealing with difficulties at work, with employees, with on-going change, and with tough decisions. (See Appendix II for a Scale designed to help highlight Values and Qualities you admire.)

This book is all about personal qualities and a personal approach to work and life. The terms contained herein can serve as a starting place and as a catalyst for creating a list of the qualities you most want to exemplify. Though we may have a general concept, delineating the most important values we have sets them firmly in our mind and establishes a base for our integrity.

The brief excerpt below from my book, *Guiding Children*, is one way we can 'get at' the qualities and values we feel are most significant in our lives. I am leaving this pretty much intact because when we consider the qualities we would like our children to have, we are essentially saying what is most important to us in our approach to life and work:

Make a short list of qualities/values that you feel you would like your child to develop. Important points to keep in mind: keep it short, less than ten items [This focuses you on the most important things. Your initial list can be much longer.]; stick to broad and general qualities and values; try to keep it focused on just qualities and values, i.e. don't put things in like, "I want my kid to be an MD," or "I want her to be a gorgeous actress."

In other words, how do you want them to be able to perceive and approach the world?

This is a developmental list. You can change it. You may remember something you forgot to add, or decide to change something later on.

As you go through the rest of this book, revise your list if something seems to 'fit' and/or write down ideas that you feel are relevant to your (child's) development as a leader as you go.

Once you have a firm foundation in what integrity and quality means to you, the real challenge is applying this to every moment of your life. Every interaction we have with others presents us with the opportunity to be 'in integrity' or to choose something else. For instance, withholding information, talking behind others' backs, criticizing, blaming, dominating or pushing your will on others, and a hundred other things probably have little to do with your list of qualities, and nothing to do with having integrity.

## How do others see us?

I truly believe that if we personally have integrity that we will honor others. However, the wise leader always considers how her/his actions and words are perceived by others. Sometimes we have to make allowances for others' perceptions even though we feel we are being completely honorable in our relations with them.

Taking the opportunity to consider our personal impact on others can be a tremendous learning tool. It also shows a great deal of understanding and caring to your fellow employees in the work place. They will more than likely sincerely appreciate your efforts and will understand more fully who you are and what you are all about. It is important to talk about what you believe in and what is important to you. People like to be informed and the more you make an effort to express your values through what you do AND what you say, the more others' will see you as the person you truly want to be.

Tell them specifically what you value and they will understand far better what integrity means to you.

> "Quality is very important to me, that is why I insist on high quality work."

> "I am very interested in what you have to say, please come to me with your suggestions. Your ideas are important to the success of this group."

> "I feel it is essential for all of us to be as open and honest with each other, if we are going to build a top-notch team."

> And so on.

Don't expect team members to just 'get it,' through your actions. Actions certainly say a great deal, but the learning curve can be very long, and difficult, especially in today's constantly changing business environment. Telling them what is important to you, coupled with your actions, gets them on board much faster.

**Respecting integrity in others**

This is all about showing your team what IS most important to you, by recognizing, verbalizing, and rewarding the behaviors and qualities you wish them to have. [And by not rewarding or recognizing those behaviors that are inappropriate.]

What we pay attention to happens!

Appreciating and recognizing integrous (this should be a word!) behavior is a very important leadership quality. Too often we spend a great deal of time paying attention to things that aren't going right. For example, a common quality of difficult people is that they seek attention by whatever means has worked for them in the past. If their actions beget attention, they are succeeding at getting what they want, even if the attention they are getting is based on their negative actions.

Pay attention to the great qualities of the members of your team every day (EVERY DAY!), and you will reinforce the values you and they need to succeed.

**Integrity is all about...**

Integrity is all about every other term in this book. It leads the list because it is the most important term in leadership. Leaders who are not 'in integrity' may have power, may 'get things done' through coercion and other negative means, and may feel important, but they are not respected.

What is most important to you?


"...there is no such thing as a minor lapse in integrity."

(Tom Peters, *Thriving on Chaos*)

# 2. Honesty**

Synonyms: guileless; straight-forward; veracious; veracity

Antonyms: dishonest; lying; underhanded; mendacious

Integrity and honesty are bedfellows. I do not believe you can have one without the other. I also believe that most of us try to be honest and open with others. Our integrity and our heart are in the right place, but it takes something a bit more to be fully honest with others. It takes self-awareness. [See Chapter 38; **Self-awareness** is also one of "The Seven Keys to Understanding and Working with Difficult People."

Honesty is one of those values that would on the surface seem to be black and white. One is honest or one is not. This may be true if we erase all other considerations and just look at the facts. However, when we look at circumstances, feelings, reactions, and a host of other elements that add to the equation, the picture becomes much grayer.

> Am I being honest if I withhold information from a colleague? Even if company policy requires that I keep this information confidential?

> Am I being honest if I tell only part of the truth and hold back some information for 'the betterment of all concerned?'

> What about 'little white lies?'

> Am I being honest if I tell the truth, but in such a way that the listener believes I am not telling the truth? Or they can't discern whether I am telling the truth or not?

> Am I being honest when I purposefully manipulate others through various tactics using information I have that gives me an edge? Even in circumstances where I mean well?

There are many ways to look at honesty and openness or as I have heard in business circles 'being transparent.' Honesty and openness are often based on judgments we make and the judgments we make, if we want to be as open and honest as possible, need to be based in self-awareness and awareness of others.

## An Example

If we look at one of the examples above – withholding information from a colleague (or friend) – we can put this into perspective.

Sometimes when we withhold information from another person it is for good reasons, either from our standpoint or from the standpoint of a third party (our team/business, etc.). E.g. One may delay the announcement of a promotion in order to facilitate the transfer of power and to help prepare people for the changes that are going to take place, or perhaps because we want the key players to be informed first.

On the surface this looks like a reasonable perspective, but what about all the people who are not being informed in the 'first wave' and yet have a large stake in what is going to happen. How do they feel while they are waiting for the axe to fall, and how will they feel when they find out about everything that has been going on behind the scenes? They probably won't feel that you, your team, or organization have been open and honest with them. They will feel disappointment, left out, 'less than,' even lied to. The question is, "Where does honesty fit into all of this?"

A good leader understands these types of concerns early on and deals with them up front. He/she pays attention to the concerns of his/her team and is aware of how people are feeling and reacting to changes that can cause difficulties. This is where openness becomes a big part of what we truly mean by being honest. Leadership means keeping people informed of everything that is possible and feasible within the scope of a given consideration. That includes, very importantly, letting them know that some information is currently confidential and that you will apprise them of the situation as it develops when you are able (allowed to) divulge further information.

People like to be kept informed even if the information is disappointing or negative. They respect those who are open about the sharing and 'not sharing' of information. They also appreciate and respect the leader who is willing to make the effort to tell them this directly without pawning it off on a subordinate.

Awareness plays a huge role in a leader's ability to be perceived as open and honest with his team members. A good leader pays attention to his team, how he comes across to his team, how they react to circumstances and to his day to day interactions with them, and to the overall openness of the group.

Important point:

**The openness and honesty of the group will often**

**(almost always)**

**reflect the leader's own approach!**

It will also reflect what you as a leader emphasize in your written and verbal communications throughout the day.

Managers often make the mistake of withholding information for any number of reasons: because it will hurt someone; because it may be perceived negatively by an individual or group; because they don't feel it is appropriate to share; or because they don't think it is important enough to share. Being honest and open means having the courage (integrity) to deal with difficult considerations by being willing to make an effort to understand and to respect the people we work with.

"Knowledge is power, but only when you spread it around."

(Dominguez)

People welcome openness. They appreciate your understanding their feelings and perspective on things. More than anything else, the people you work with value your willingness to be as honest and open as possible considering the circumstances.

"Honesty isn't the best policy; it is the only policy."

**\*\*Honesty** is one of "The Seven Keys to Understanding and Working with Difficult People." (Koob)

# 3. Trust

Synonyms: confide in; have confidence in; rely on; faith; believe; entrust

Antonyms: doubt; mistrust; disbelieve; distrust; suspect; disbelieve

"A Scout is Trustworthy..."

[I think it is interesting that Trust is the first of the Boy Scout Laws. [along with, Loyal, Helpful, Friendly, Courteous, Kind, Obedient, Cheerful, Thrifty, Brave, Clean, and Reverent.]

To be trusted by another person is one of the most significant things we can accomplish in life. It is also one of the most difficult things, especially for leaders, to achieve with others.

Trust comes from and develops from our integrity and honesty. However, while our attitude is critical to the eventual development of trust with the people we work with and for, it is only part of the whole picture. Everyone we interact with brings another figure to the equation.

Trust is affected a great deal by people's experiences. Untrusting relationships they may have had with other leaders and other difficult situations (especially leadership change) can affect them for some time. For some it is easy to trust an open, honorable leader; for others, trust takes considerable effort and time on the leader's part to develop.

We could take almost all the terms in the rest of this book and use them as inspiration for our work with others. In doing so, we would probably develop a tremendous amount of trust, respect, and honesty with most of our compatriots. Though we will talk about each of these terms in turn, here are a few that I feel highlight the development of trust in others.

# Key Ideas for being Trustworthy

## Trust and respect others

A leader has to be the catalyst for a trusting relationship with his team. You can hope it will work the other way naturally because you ARE trustworthy, but it probably won't, not for everyone.

## Appreciate and recognize others

Openly and regularly appreciating others is plain good sense. When we appreciate and recognize other people, they notice. It is perhaps the most fundamental need of people in a work environment (and in life!). We all want to feel needed and useful, and it is great when that is recognized by significant people in our lives.

## Care

People want to feel cared for. It doesn't necessarily have to be 'touchy/feely.' A sense that you care about them and their concerns goes a long way. It has to do with respectful attention, and can be as simple as remembering details about them and what is important to them.

## Connectedness

Being available and visible is paramount to good leadership. "Office managers," those who remain in their offices, are not leaders at all. To be true leaders we need to get out and be with people. It is all about having a good sense and feeling of what is happening 'out there' in the trenches.

## Passion

If you are passionate about what you do, it will translate to others. It may take time for the reluctant ones, but it does happen.

## Time

Building trust in an organization and with all of the people up and down the chain takes time. You can figure on at least six months if you are doing all the right things, and up to two years or more for the 'stubborn ones.' Everyone is different. Most will come around when they are ready. However, keep in mind that your trust of them, your respect for who they are and what they are capable of, must come first. Give them the honor of trusting them and they will most often return the favor.

A good exercise to consider is to read and review all the other concepts in this book, and then come back to this chapter. Briefly consider the impact each of these has on developing trust within your work relationships. Key ideas relevant to your working with your team may leap out at you as you go through this process.

**Trusting Yourself**

It would seem that this would be a 'no-brainer,' but our own self-worth, self-respect, and self-awareness play a huge role in who we are as a leader. At the deepest roots of who we are we need to have a fundamental trust in ourselves: our abilities; the truth of who we are and what we believe in; our feelings; and our ability to control ourselves in difficult situations when we need to. Leadership is often about how we come across to others in the most stressful of times.

This book is about self-awareness and learning better who we are so that we can work with our strengths and think about and develop those areas we feel less comfortable and confident about. It is also about self-renewal – we can all use support and encouragement as we work with all the things that impact us at work and in life.

Holding on to the truth of who you are is the foundation for building trust throughout your life.

# 4. Ownership

Synonyms: possession; having; claim; proprietorship; responsible for; accountable; dominion

Antonyms: not own up to; be irresponsible; blame; complain

### Do you own your own life?

This is an excellent question to ask because it is easy to get caught up in the strivings and stress of our every day work load and not pay attention to what is really important – owning who we are and what we are all about. The best way to answer this question is to ask yourself two other questions:

> When things happen in life are you prone to look outside yourself and blame circumstances, other people, your boss, your employer/business,...'them?

> Do you recognize that your life is YOUR life and when stuff happens, you have to adjust and make changes so you can successfully tackle the challenges that come your way?

Great leaders don't look over their shoulder or point to others or circumstances for excuses for their failure or success in work and in life. They ask themselves the question, "What can **I** change to find a solution to this concern?" Whether it is a major disruption at work or simply a disgruntled employee; leaders seek solutions.

Leaders don't:

> Blame

> Point Fingers

> Criticize

> Back stab

> Take credit for others' work

Whine and moan about 'circumstances'

Say 'Yeah but....' [Offer excuses] to/for everything.

Ownership has been at the top of my list of important words for the last few years. I ask myself this question frequently:

> "When it is all said and done do you want your life
>
> to be about a bunch of excuses?"

If a co-worker is not doing their job, is not a team player, and is creating angst and division on our team, we can choose to blame him/her, offer them up as an excuse for what is not getting done, moan, whine, and worry; or we can 'own' the situation and find ways to make changes:

> Leaders motivate.
>
> Leaders make decisions that better their team.
>
> Leaders create and offer training.
>
> Leaders find the right niche for a player.
>
> Leaders work with a team member to improve their attitude and skills.
>
> Leaders make hard choices when they have to.
>
> Leaders DO.

Great leaders take responsibility for themselves and for their teams. They even shoulder responsibilities where others have dropped the ball because it is what is best for them, their team, and their business, AND because it is the right thing to do. Leaders get things done because they are willing to step up to the plate again and again in spite of whether they struck out the previous time or the previous five times. They recognize that ownership means making a difference.

**Excuses are easy**

Leading isn't always easy, but it is a heck of a lot more rewarding, when we are committed to doing it right.

We take pride in something when we are invested in what it is all about. Tom Peters and Nancy Austin quote an NCO from Gen. Bill Creech's command, "General, when's the last time you washed a rental car?" (*A Passion for Excellence*) The point being that we don't own a rental car. We are not invested in what it is and how it looks, only in what it does for us. When we don't own it, we don't take care of it – we don't keep it clean.

**Investment/ownership means we care**

Taking ownership of your own life means: teamwork; not blaming others; nipping worry in the bud and dealing with what comes up, not what might come up; finding solutions instead of complaining; and eliminating excuses from your vocabulary.

If you have lost your job, or done lousy work and been reprimanded, you can choose to blame the company, an individual, and/or the world at large. You can choose to bemoan your fate and complain to everyone who will listen. You can choose to worry day in and day out about everything that is happening. You can choose to be a negative drain on all those people you contact throughout the day.

Or you can choose to be more positive and proactive.

[See Appendix III, "Choices," A short perspective on the Choices we can make every day.]

Ownership doesn't just mean being part of a team,

**it means being the team**

and exemplifying to everyone what being part of a team means.

Take ownership of your work and life – be a part of your team; **be the team**; BE YOUR TEAM!

# 5. Accountable

Synonyms: answerable; responsible

Antonyms: irresponsible; passing the buck

Typically when we think of being accountable we think of the types of things we need to produce to fulfill the requirements and expectations of our job. You are accountable for bringing a certain number of widgets forward in the production line, or for "X" dollars in sales, or for training so many people. You may also be accountable for a budget, planning and strategy, hiring and firing, etc. Accountability has to do with outcomes.

Accountability has often been raised as an issue in education as well as business. Teachers need to be accountable for the learning imparted to their students. From a 'governmental' or 'accountability' perspective this usually means how they train the students to do well on a selected set of standardized tests. In other words do the students meet a certain criteria (outcome) that is set as a norm for your school, state, region, country.

A good teacher knows that true accountability means they are concerned with every student's growth, learning, involvement, excitement about learning in general, and a student's overall appreciation of the world, others, and life. It sounds like a huge responsibility – and it is.

A good leader knows he/she shoulders much more in the sense of what they are accountable for than just work outcomes or output.

A good leader should recognize his/her 'accountability' for:

> every other word in this book and then some.

Here are some highlighted considerations:

> Education, Training, Growth of team members

> Recognition, Appreciation, Support

Care, Compassion, Well-being

Motivation, Self-respect, Loyalty, Pride

Passion, Vision, Quality, Initiative

A great leader knows that she must also be accountable for all of these things for HERSELF!

Our concern for others will only have a marked impact if we first take care of our own business. We must be accountable for ourselves, to ourselves, for who we are and what we bring to the workplace. It is about self-worth and self-confidence and about understanding who we are and what we do (self-awareness, identity). [See Chapter Seven]

Leading is a tremendous responsibility.

# 6. Responsibility

Synonyms: duty; obligation; subject to; faithfulness; steadfastness

Antonyms: untrustworthy; irresponsible; exception

Being responsible is part of ownership. It is a word that goes considerably beyond the typical connotation that we are accountable for something or "responsible" for "X" project, or "Y's" work, or the output of our team. Responsibility implies that we owe something to someone, that we have an obligation, a debt, or a duty. I like Robert Heinlein's perspective:

> "Do not confuse 'duty' with what other people expect of you; they are utterly different. Duty is a debt that you owe yourself to fulfill the obligations you have assumed voluntarily....the reward is self-respect....let the choice be yours. Don't do it because it is 'expected' of you." (*Time Enough for Love*)

Leadership has many responsibilities. Our greatest responsibility, however, is to our self. We cannot lead effectively unless we are comfortable with who we are and what we are striving for.

When we really think about it, we cannot assume responsibility FOR another person. They have their own life to live and their own ownership of their life and work. We can help and support others and as a leader we can take responsibility for their actions. We cannot take responsibility for their life.

We can, however, as a leader be responsible for, if we choose, all that leadership implies.

The most important consideration is that we choose the role of responsibility as part of who we are as a person and as a leader. "Assuming" responsibility is an interesting way of phrasing the myriad of things that we take on as a manager or leader that need to get done or we need to be concerned with. These can range from our employees well being, to their roles and productivity, to a product or service, to final outcomes and rewards.

However, I believe that taking responsibility implies, for the true leader, a deeper level of commitment than just outcomes. It means that we are involved in the development of a true sense of ownership for our team. Responsibility in this sense is a passion and vision for what CAN BE, and doing our best to instill that passion and vision in the people we work with on a day-to-day basis. It goes beyond being responsible for some outcome, and it becomes a shared involvement in the process and commitment of getting there.

Process is an ongoing, forward-moving, action-oriented concept. When people are involved and responsible for the process, reaching a goal becomes a celebration of what has led up to the outcome. The process is our true responsibility because it is the most fundamental and by far the most extensive part of our work life.

When we take on a leadership role, we can choose to take on a dynamic, constantly changing responsibility of involving our team in not only reaching point "A," but owning and being excited about getting there. If and when we reach this stage, our responsibility for outcomes becomes a much smaller part of our team's focus. It also means that we can focus on our true responsibilities of taking care of and appreciating our team members and, very importantly, taking care of ourselves.

Keep this in mind: Everyone is always responsible for themselves. Leaders, however, are also responsible in many ways for others!

# 7. Reliability

Synonyms: dependability

Antonyms: unreliable; undependable

Reliability isn't just about being on time, it is about being there for people. It has a lot to do with trust. If a new leader wants to develop trust with her team members she needs to cultivate reliability in everything she does as one of her primary virtues.

Poor leaders spend a great deal of time worrying about the appearance of being reliable up the chain of command. Great leaders are concerned about being reliable for their team.

Being reliable goes a long way with other people. When people can count on you to take action on what you say you will, be open and honest about what you can't do, and keep them informed as much as possible about everything that impacts them, you will develop a deeper commitment and loyalty from them.

> Being reliable means being in contact with your team members on a regular basis and listening to their concerns and ideas.

> Being reliable means accomplishing what you say you will AND admitting what you can't.

> Being reliable means caring about more than just the job they are doing; it means caring about them and who they are and what is important to them.

Ask yourself this question: "What does it mean when I say, 'He's reliable'?"

> "You can count on him."

> "He shoots straight from the hip."

> "He will do anything for you."

> "He cares about how I am doing."

"He's there when you need him."

"I feel comfortable asking him questions."

"If I need something, he will let me know what he can do."

"He's a regular, 'Joe.'"

"He doesn't mince words."

"He will do what he says he will do, or tell you why he can't."

"He keeps us informed."

Be there for your people. It will pay huge dividends in every aspect of your work life!

# 8. Self-control**

Synonyms: willpower; self-discipline; self-command; restraint; self-will; stability

Antonyms: unrestrained; free; wild; uncontrolled; intractable

"Because we mistake what is impermanent to be permanent,

we suffer."

(Pema Chodron)

In working through many books on change over the past year and a half, I have come to realize how important this concept is to keeping a perspective on everything that happens to us in life.

We want to control a great deal of what happens to us and around us. We want things to be permanent and not to change. We want to control things so that there is stability in our lives and work. The reality is far different. In truth we control very little, and there is very little in life that is truly permanent. Control yourself – it is a much happier and healthier way of being with the world.

Ask yourself these next two questions. Take some time to ponder your answers. Then make a list of your responses. If you do this exercise, you will learn a lot about how you really interact with the world around you:

What do I control?

What don't I control?

Control is an illusion. Control of others is an illusion of the power-hungry and of those who have little self-worth. It is driven by ego. Trying to control others is stupid – it always results in a negative reaction in the short or long terms by the person or people one is trying to control.

---

One of my readers brought to my attention the military concept of 'command and control.' From my point of view this type of leadership is no different from a 'control' perspective of any business or organization. Good military leadership focuses on teamwork. A good commander not only expects his team to obey orders and follow regulations for the best possible outcome, but also inculcates the value-added quality of intelligent decision-making when it is needed. (And it IS often needed out in the field and in combat.)

Discipline is self-control. The military uses discipline as a means of training soldiers to be members of a team – so that they develop esprit de corps, they learn specific abilities and responses that can save them and their team members' lives, to boost comaderery, etc. Poor leaders, military or otherwise, expect blind obedience to a set of rules and regulations. Having been in the Air Force and known Army officers throughout my life while growing up with my career military dad, I have known both types: rigid, inflexible 'leaders,' and those who instilled in their men and women true control – self-control. The latter were the real leaders.

Self-control is the only control that a leader has or needs. When we control ourselves we inspire self-control in others. Telling, ordering, strict adherence to restrictive rules, and forcing others marks the manager who has no other means to motivate his team and whose self-worth is very shaky. Leaders ask, inquire, share, become involved, learn with, and generally exhibit behaviors that stimulate people to do their best because they know that self-control works.

We wish for so many things to be 'permanent,' but in reality very little is.

In the lobby of University Administration buildings there are often pictures of all the past presidents lining the walls. Many of their contributions and even their impact have long been forgotten and at some time, perhaps in the distant or not so distant future, that auditorium, those pictures, and that University will be no more than piles of dust ready to begin anew. All that they 'controlled' soon will be long gone. However, it is very likely that those few,

22

those who were first and foremost in control of who they were and how they impacted the world around them, had a lasting effect on the people who worked with them. That kind of effect continues on and on, in and through the lives we have influenced.

What is permanent is what we carry through ourselves from moment to moment and the precious gifts we give to others from and during those moments. That is true control – controlling what we do and how we impact others and the world around us. We have that choice – perhaps in this moment, or the next, or, maybe we just missed a moment. (Maybe we will do better with the next one.)

We can always choose to exercise self-control.


The wise leader exercises a lot.


** **Self-Control** is one of "The Seven Keys to Understanding and Working with Difficult People." (Koob).

# 9. Loyalty

Synonyms: allegiance; faithfulness; fidelity; trustworthy; conscientious; dependability

Antonyms: unfaithful; infidelity; untrustworthy; disloyalty

Loyalty is DEAD!

Or so it would seem in today's business environment. Gone are the days when employees remained with a company for decades, retired after forty-some years, and got a firm handshake, gold watch, and thanks from the president of the firm. Today it is much more likely that an employee will change jobs at least several times while moving up the chain, and in more than a few cases, talented employees will move within a few years to greener pastures.

> How can businesses and teams survive with this type of turnover?

> How do they deal with a world where loyalty is measured by a different yardstick than it was thirty years ago?

## Loyalty is all about ATTITUDE!

Leaders, great leaders, have the attitude that what they are doing NOW is what deserves the utmost effort and focus. What this means in plain language is that if I am working for Microsoft, I give my all to Microsoft up until I leave that playing field for my new job at Dell. Once I am at Dell, I will become immersed in that job and that culture and bring everything I have to succeeding in my new environs.

Great leaders inspire the same kind of attitude and hence loyalty in their teams. They do it through a fundamental belief that they can make a difference. They do it through example.

They assume responsibility immediately for what they bring to the job. There is a dogged deterministic attitude about getting things done and getting things done right. They know that no matter how difficult or trying the situation or the transition, they will dive in with everything they have and make the most of what they are given.

There are many examples of good leaders throughout the business literature that reflect this type of loyalty and determination from the get-go. When I read Lou Gertstner's book, *Who Says Elephants Can't Dance*, I was impressed by his determination to succeed and his loyalty and commitment to doing his best for IBM. Lou turned IBM around during the 1980s and 1990s, and while he was apprehensive before and after taking on this immense job, you can sense that as soon as he made a decision, he was committed to doing his utmost for IBM and the many people there. I also feel this same current of loyalty and determinism underlies the executives of the companies described in Jim Collins' book, *Good to Great*.

Loyalty is something YOU bring to the equation. It is your personal commitment to your work and life. Get it, keep it. It will have a marked impact on the loyalty of the members of your team.

# 10. Committed

Synonyms: dedicated; devoted; invested in; responsible for; persevering; persistent

Antonyms: uncommitted; undecided; irresponsible

I think the word committed has a bit more activity to it than 'commitment.' It also is a word that furthers the notion of Loyalty. A good leader is committed to what he is doing – his work.

We spend a tremendous amount of time and effort in our work lives. The forty-hour work week is a dream world for most managers. It is far more likely that a dedicated leader is spending sixty or more hours a week at the office, and more time working at home on the computer, traveling, and talking on a cell phone.

Being committed to your work is more than going to a job. There is something about their job that a true leader loves. It isn't power, because that is essentially ephemeral. It isn't control of others, money, or a process.

I sincerely believe it is 'the doing,' the involvement in something that we feel will make a difference.

Leaders make a difference because they are committed to making a difference.

Managers push things around, put things in order, make sure things go smoothly, keep people in line. Unless they take the huge step forward into leadership – being committed to making a difference – they will always be a manager. The difference isn't in a position or in the power one has, it is in how one approaches their work, their job, and their life.

I have observed and coached many managers, directors, senior directors, vice-presidents, and CEO's. The good and great leaders stand out because they have that something extra that could be defined in various ways. Take any of the highlighted terms in this book and you will begin to define great leadership. But when one comes down to brass tacks it is not just about what they do, who they do it with, how much their team produces, who likes them or doesn't like them, or a host of other things, it is about <u>how</u> they approach their job. How they commit to their own excellence and to developing the excellence of others. They are committed to doing well.

> What drives a leader to always strive for personal excellence?

Psychologically one could make an attempt to define this in terms of behaviors and causes for behaviors. The truth is, if you take any great leader and compare them to another great leader, their experiences, background, motivation, etc. is vastly different. Great leaders lead differently from each other, but at the root is something that separates them from the average manager.

Observe a great leader; read what they have written or what others have written about them. Take a careful look at how they approach their work and their lives in general. Simply put, great leaders are committed and you see it in how they approach their work on a day to day, moment to moment, interaction to interaction basis.

It is a commitment to HOW you do things, not what you do, that is so important.

# 11. Conscientious

Synonyms: principled; assiduous; persevering

Antonyms: careless; unscrupulous; uncaring; underhanded

Con-sci-en-tious: 1. Governed by, or made or done according to, what one knows is right; scrupulous; honest 2. Showing care and precision; painstaking [Webster's New World Dictionary]

> Carol: "How do you spell conscience?...
>
> Carol's Mother: "c-o-n-s-c-i-e-n-c-e."
>
> Carol: "Con – **science**?...That doesn't sound right."
>
> (from the film *As Good As It Gets* with Helen Hunt and Jack Nicholson, Brooks, 1997)

When I think of 'Conscience' I remember the cartoons I saw when I was a kid, where there was a little angel sitting on a man's shoulder (and often a little devil lurking nearby).

Conscientious, however, is a more dynamic word. It puts 'conscience' into motion and makes it my responsibility. Conscience is not outside oneself. It is part of who we are, fundamentally. It is about the choices **we** make from moment to moment because of who we are. The little angel and devil are not outside forces that impinge on us and influence our decisions in life. Our conscientiousness comes from our commitment to what we believe in and it is rooted in our ability to control ourselves.

There is something special about conscientious leaders. I believe it has to do with caring. It is something that goes a step or two beyond the Webster definition above. It is not just about doing what is right, being scrupulous, and being honest. A conscientious person **cares** about doing what is right, doing their job well, taking care of the people they work with, and putting their best into everything they tackle.

Conscientious people don't always do the right thing. They aren't perfect. They make plenty of mistakes – but they try! And when they make a mistake or fail in an endeavor, they are willing to admit where they have fallen short and will make every effort to make amends. They don't hide behind excuses or point their fingers at others. And, they are willing to learn from their mistakes!

When it comes to responsibility, the buck stops with them.

# 12. Credible

Synonyms: dependable; reliable; sincere/sincerity; believable

Antonyms: unreliable; dishonest; undependable

Credibility goes a step further than honesty. It has to do with perception. I might perceive my interactions with others to be totally above board and rooted in my fundamental belief in being honest with others. However, that may not be how I am seen by the people I work with.

This is particularly true during times of change.

If an organization is going through significant change, credibility – the perception of how honest everyone perceives their leaders (and organization) to be, is a huge factor in how bumpy the road may be in moving ahead. A new leader entering an intact team or organization with a long history has many issues to deal with before people will consider him/her trustworthy and credible.

Openness is one of the key tools a leader has in developing his/her credibility within an organization. When people feel they are kept informed, and most especially kept informed about changes that are taking place or will take place, they are more likely to begin to accept a new and different leadership approach. It is also critical **to be open** to one's team **about what cannot be shared** because of confidentiality or timing issues.

People, all of us, appreciate the effort to keep us on board and up-to-date on what is transpiring. One of the most common errors in leading teams and organizations through change is the failure to share information when it can be shared, AND to let people know when information can't be shared and why.

Often people will associate reliability with one's credibility. Great leaders do what they say they will do or let people know why they can't. Poor leaders ignore people's concerns and desire to know, and bury disappointments or failures through deceptive practices. Poor leaders manipulate others by playing games with information, talking and working behind the scenes, and making decisions that impact their players without considering how it will impact them and without letting them in on the decision-making process.

Like trust, credibility takes time to develop. Working closely with people, staying receptive to ideas, communicating and sharing your own vision, method, and passion, and helping team players be involved in important decision-making processes, will help bring your team members around.

It is worth the effort. Committed and loyal employees will be the result.

# 13. Stability

Synonyms: steadiness; durability, solidity; resoluteness

Antonyms: unrest; change; impermanence

Today's business environment is anything but stable. A leader who is attached solely to things remaining the same or 'business as usual' is going to quickly lose his footing and be swallowed up in the fast pace of change. Stability is the last thing we want in a global change-orientated economy.

Or is it?

Stability in leadership serves as a rock upon which people can rely during the constantly shifting environment that business finds as the norm today. Leaders, as we shall see later in this book, must support and exemplify innovation, creativity, flexibility, and experimentation. However, they must also provide a center to which team members can come to retain their focus and sense of having control of all that is transpiring around them.

Stability, first and foremost, comes from a leader's self-control. In spite of all that impacts their team and themselves on a daily basis they represent a foundation for others to follow. Rather than being set adrift by changes and difficulties, a good leader finds ways to deal with these types of issues from the foundation of self that he/she brings to the table.

Demeanor is a key issue in maintaining a sense of stability. While major change and other difficult situations affect all members of a team emotionally, physically, intellectually, and spiritually in the broadest sense of the word, the great leaders maintain control of themselves and the appearance they present to others. A wise leader knows when to show emotion and when to show a stalwart persona in the face of problems and difficulties. A good leader provides what the team needs:

Sometimes team members need reassurances

Sometimes they need strength.

Sometimes they need a kind and caring mentor.

Sometimes they need someone being honest with them.

Sometimes they need to know where they stand.

Sometimes they need someone to talk to.

Sometimes they need to be kept informed.

Sometimes they simply need to be appreciated.


Stability in leadership in the best sense of the word is about 'being there' when people need you to be – being the bulwark upon which they can come to when the times are tough. It is about them knowing you are available IF they need you when the world and how they deal with it is in constant flux.


Provide stability when it is needed

# 14. Continuity

Synonyms: constancy; persistence; flow; endure

Antonyms: inconstant; disruption; interruption

Continuity is closely related to stability. When we have things that remain the same, solid, in our work and life, we will be able to handle much that impacts us.

A good leader can help his/her team or organization maintain stability through significant change and through difficulties by providing for as much continuity as possible during the process. This may take many forms:

> Maintaining open lines of communication with all team members
>
> Establishing patterns of action (strategy, planning, procedures) that help team members orient while maintaining the ability to react flexibly when needed
>
> Encouraging information sharing across matrixes and lines
>
> Recognizing and celebrating progress throughout the change process
>
> Incrementalizing change – providing for acceptance of degrees or stages throughout the change process so that everyone has the opportunity to become acclimated before moving ahead
>
> Holding on to structures and mementoes of the past as the team works through change.
>
> Providing support and training throughout the change process
>
> Being open to and encouraging ideas and suggestions from everyone on the team.

Maintaining members' focus on the values and outcomes that create the team's vision

When we have continuity in some aspects of our work environment it is far easier to deal with other things that are in a state of flux. Good leaders recognize that change takes time and effort. It takes leading people forward while maintaining links to the past and to the ties that bond a group together.

Continuity means having something (and someone) that provides us with stability through change.

Continuity implies sameness AND motion. It is an interesting and powerful combination.

# 15. Disciplined

Synonyms: under control; conduct; orderliness; trained

Antonyms: out of control; uncontrolled; disorderly

"You cannot control others; you can only control yourself."

(*Understanding and Working with Difficult People*," Koob)

"The first person you lead is you."

(Maxwell, *The 21 Indispensible...*)

Not all leaders are well organized. I would warrant though, that the best ones work at it diligently and/or have others around them that make up for their weakness in this area. Some great leaders are fairly disorganized, but they know exactly how much freedom they can get away with before it becomes a problem.

While a good leader may or may not be an organizational wizard, a disciplined leader controls himself, not necessarily his work environment or others. In controlling himself, he exemplifies what he expects from his coworkers and team members. There is no compromise in this quality of discipline.

A leader must maintain control. Whatever strong emotions and reactions one may feel, it is important to contain these when dealing and working with others. Explosive outbursts have no place in the work environment.

This does not mean that leaders cannot express how they feel. Wise leaders, however, express their emotions while in complete control, and as kindly as possible. I once read a statement, I believe it was from a master violin teacher, that essentially said, "I never get angry with a student when I am actually angry. I only show them that I am upset when I am in control of my feelings."

There is a lot of wisdom in this statement. Sometimes we do need to let a person know how we feel, but expressing that feeling through an uncontrolled reaction doesn't do anyone any good. It can be very detrimental to establishing a trusting, credible relationship with an employee. It can also throw tremendous problems into the path of trying to help and develop a low-achieving or unmotivated employee.

When we can respond to others from a confident, self-controlled stance that is anchored in our own self-worth we can provide feedback, support, and understanding that will yield much more positive results. People do not appreciate being disciplined, but they do appreciate a disciplined person working with them to alleviate concerns.

Questions we should ask ourselves every day:

> "How am I interacting with others"

> "How does what I say and do impact others?"

> "Am I maintaining control when things are not going well?"

> "Does each interaction I have with a team member have value for me and for them?"

> "How can I add value to everyone I see today?"

# 16. Humility

Synonyms: humble; modest; self-effacing; unassuming

Antonyms: pride; vainglory; conceit; egotistic

Great business leaders are not pompous. They do not have big egos, nor do they have a need to draw attention to themselves constantly. The truly great leaders lead from an inner strength that brooks no nonsense, but at the same time they don't need to broadcast their position and power. If we look back at some of the great leaders from this country: Abraham Lincoln, John F. Kennedy, Robert E. Lee, and many more, we can see their strength of purpose, their resolve, and their duty.

What leaders do you admire in the business world? Within your own organization? Do they dominate meetings? Have to have the last word? Are they inflexible to others' ideas if they contrast with their own? Do they railroad their pet projects through the system? Do they take credit for other peoples' ideas or for successes from within the company? Do you have any sense that they place themselves above you or others?

Great leaders:

> Listen to others

> Let others win

> Offer credit to others and take responsibility for concerns and problems themselves

> Have a quiet strength that leads by example

> Support and encourage the team and the team members

Being humble or modest doesn't mean that the good leader lets other people roll all over them or allows others to always have their own way. It means that they listen, inform, and work from their strengths, they acknowledge and work on their weaknesses, and they care about the people they work with. Leaders have a tremendous amount of inner strength. They have and work constantly toward a set of personal values, as well as support and encourage the values and goals of their team members. Because of this they can work, in essence, from the sidelines and be satisfied that true valor and pride comes from what their team has accomplished.

They are who they are and it is enough.

# 17. Idealism

Synonyms:  high-mindedness;  noble-mindedness;  principle; conscience; exalted; lofty; utopian

Antonyms: ignoble; lowly; base; dystopian


If one goes by the literature of the past several hundred years, one would find that the ideal or utopian society is a great idea, but it doesn't quite work out that way, at least not for everyone. There are, in the final analysis losers as well as winners. It is easy to recall the 'utopian' society of Orwell's, *Animal Farm.*

Though idealistic, ideal, and utopian seem to have acquired a bit of a negative tinge to them, I still believe that a good leader has at his/her roots a solid core of beliefs and values that form the elements of a broad perspective of what they are all about. They bring this foundation with them to the workplace in the form of a personal vision of what they believe work and life can be.

While utopia may not exist in any workplace or with any workforce, a leader has a belief that it is worth aiming at/working toward. It is not so important that one reaches this type of goal, but that the goal is worth striving toward. A clear personal vision (see Chapter 88, on "Vision") enables a manager to lead through example and with a passion for doing things right. With 'right' being their personal vision of the ideal work environment for all concerned.

Is there a right way to lead?

Is there a perfect environment for a business or team?

Probably not, because everyone's personal vision of perfection is vastly different. What makes the difference between a leader and a follower or a great leader and a so-so leader is that they empower themselves **and others** to strive for what they each believe in.

One of my ideals may be to 'get things done,' to move ahead and create as much as possible within the shortest period of time so that our team/business stays on the cutting edge of its field. A co-leader or another team member may be focused on 'getting things right,' dotting all the 'i's' and crossing all the 't's.' They make sure everything is as close to perfection as possible. These are vastly different visions of what is 'right' or ideal and can lead to tremendous concerns in the workplace. Rather than have differences in personal vision cause disruptions on a team, a leader can complement his own vision of getting things done by taking advantage of his co-worker's focus of getting things right.

A good leader will utilize the best everyone has to offer, each person's ideals and strengths, and use those within the structure of his own personal vision to create the 'best of all possible worlds.' (*Candide*, Voltaire)

The best of all possible worlds is not what I want or what you want but what works for who we are within the scope of what we need to accomplish. It is attainable only through quality leadership and striving – through a leader's ability to bring personal focus to their work and to lead by example.

Great leaders know themselves. They can take a list of values, qualities, ideals (as in this book) and delineate exactly which ideas are most important to them, where their strengths are, what their weaknesses are, and then use that knowledge to improve themselves and also use them as a driving motivation to build the best possible team/organization. [See Appendices I and II for Scales developed for this purpose.]

Good leaders don't impose their ideals on others. They lead by letting the people they work with know what is of value to them. If **Quality** is one paramount factor in their perfect world, then they talk, walk, breathe, and do quality at all times. Team players understand from the get-go that this is a top priority for their manager. The team leader doesn't have to force quality down their throats, his/her whole being says quality is important, and that kind of passion and effort rubs off.

If **Integrity** is another fundamental value, then great leaders inculcate that into everything they do and with every person they interact with. They will accept nothing less from themselves. Their team members will quickly understand that it is expected of them as well. It will become a part of the team because it is highly valued. As the team rallies around the banner of integrity, those who don't will find themselves out in left field looking in.

Idealism in this sense is about what you believe in – your core. It can become the core or foundation for your team as well, as long as there is flexibility for others to have their own values. What becomes honored is the value each person adds to the team.

Live the life and work you dream to live. It is much more likely to become reality and you will have become a true leader in the process.

# PART II

# SERVICE to Others

A leader is a…

"relentless architect of the possibilities of human beings."

(Benjamin Zander, conductor, Boston Philharmonic,
quoted by Peters, *The Circle of Innovation*,)

"The most important measure of how good a game I played

was how much better I'd made my teammates play."

(Bill Russell, NBA Star, quoted by Maxwell,
*The 17 Indisputable Laws of Teamwork*)

# 18. Service

Synonyms: help; duty; assist; assistance; cooperation; aid

Antonyms: disservice; ill-turn

To provide service to others is the noblest of professions. How we perceive our service to others is an essential part of good leadership.

A waitress or a clerk serves others. As a part of his/her service he/she always has the opportunity to have and make a positive impact on a person's day. That is not only a big responsibility, it is the essence of humanity. When we perceive our life and work as service to others and can keep that in the forefront as we work, we have immediately changed our whole perspective on what we do and how we do it.

Good leaders serve the people they work with and work for. Most importantly they serve the people who work for them.

It is important to consider that the majority of businesses today have a major part of their business in the service sector. Production is no longer the dominant industry and if one puts only a slight twist to one's perspective, the development and producing of all products is service-oriented as well.

Service to others is about honoring their humanity. We can choose a host of ways to interact with people – centered in the positive, the negative, or in neutrality. This whole section of this book delineates ways in which we can make service a part of our leadership style. It pays huge dividends in how the people you work with take personal ownership in how they approach their work and you, and their responsibility for their own success.

When I conceive of my role as a supervisor of others from a service perspective, I create a different approach and aura about my work with others. I see my work, their work, and our efforts together in a completely different light. Yes, power can corrupt, and any boss or manager in essence has power over others. How we think about that responsibility equates to how we handle it.

When I gave up a leadership role I had for several years and was moving into a new phase of my life, it was fascinating to stand back, mentally and emotionally, and observe how that felt. There were definitely aspects of the 'power' of that position that I missed. I was able to learn a great deal about how to look at power and service to others as a result.

I believe it is a disservice to the people we work with up and down the chain, to see our relationship in any other light. As you read through the other chapters in this section keep this broad concept of Service in mind. You will recognize how important this idea is in building a dynamic, productive, happy team, as well as in establishing successful relationships throughout your work and life.

Service is the number one job in America.

Service should be your top priority for your employees, co-workers, bosses, and customers. It should also be the top priority of your employees, co-workers, bosses, and customers.

Service is about how we interact with others.

Service IS who you are if you are a leader.

# 19. Appreciation

Synonyms: thankfulness; admiration; gratefulness; acknowledgment; recognition

Antonyms: ungratefulness, ingratitude

"The deepest human need is to be appreciated."

(William James, psychologist)

We all like to be appreciated for who we are and for what we do. It doesn't matter what level we are in an organization. It is amazing how easy this is to forget. Mid-level managers focus on getting things done, keeping things running and organized, and producing, producing, producing. Vice presidents, presidents, CEOs and CFOs get wrapped up in administration, budgetary and personnel concerns. Workers seem to think that managers sit in their ivory towers reaping the benefits of their hard-earned labor. They often believe their leaders are enjoying the good life of golf, dinners, and privileges with no need to be recognized in any other way.

The truth is most people work pretty hard. Unfortunately there are always a very few at all levels that don't. We all need to be appreciated whatever level we are at or whatever rank we hold. It IS that fundamental to our existence and well being.

Appreciation is simple. It is one of the easiest gifts we can offer another human being, and so often we let these golden opportunities slip by. It costs us nothing financially, and very little in time and effort. It is amazing the benefits that grow from such a simple gesture.

My proudest effort as a manager was in turning around a department that was literally loathed by the rest of the organization when I took over the helm. I certainly made some mistakes in the position, and learned a tremendous amount as a result. However, one thing I did do right was appreciate people, and what they did for me and my department.

Mostly I did it in small ways:

"Thank You" is a HUGE phrase.

I thanked people for the smallest effort and response to requests. I did it personally – for instance, a simple statement to a worker in my building or a small gift for someone who had done some extra work for me. I never farmed this stuff off to my administrative assistant or to another member of my team. I would also grab the phone even before a task was completed and call a supervisor in another area and thank them for getting to the job quickly. And I always followed up with an e-mail, note, or formal memo.

It took awhile for people to realize I was sincere and that this wasn't just a short-lived tactic. By the time I left that position I had developed a positive working relationship with all the areas and teams my department had contact with, from custodial to building maintenance to the senior administration.

Appreciation is one of the most fundamental needs we all have. When I think back on the best work experiences of my life, the ones that stand out, by far, are those where people told me that they really appreciated what I had done for them.

The best way to do this is to get in the habit of saying it.

"I appreciated your fixing that broken machine so quickly."

"It really made a difference to our team's success when you got through with that report on time and gave us feedback quickly."

"I wanted you to know that I have appreciated your hard work on this project."

"I really appreciate your openness and willingness to mentor me."

"Thanks for being here. You've made a big difference to this team and to me."

All people appreciate being appreciated. For some people it is what they need more than anything else to make them a viable and productive team member. Don't forget to appreciate everyone 'up,' 'down,' and 'across' the chain.

> It has to be sincere and heartfelt.

> It shouldn't be or sound obsequious.

> It is best if it is done spontaneously, and as soon as possible.

> If you want to be successful, appreciate everyone.

There are always things you can find to acknowledge about a person and their work. There are a zillion ways. Get in the habit!

A question that an employee asks every day, many times a day, in many different ways:

## Am I valued?

Ask yourself this question every day, many times a day:

## Do my employees know that I value them?

# 20. Acknowledgment

Synonyms: endorsement; recognition; response; support; vote of thanks; avowal

Antonyms: disavow; deny; not notice

Acknowledgment is perhaps even more fundamental to self-worth than appreciation. We want to be acknowledged for being. We want to be acknowledged for who we are as individuals, despite our foibles. We want to be acknowledged for our effort, our work.

Tom Peters (with Nancy Austin in *A Passion for Excellence*) talks about MBWA – Management By Wandering Around – in a number of his works (see bibliography). The idea is not new; it has been written about using a wide variety of approaches for years. The problem is that it isn't being done nearly enough! [My take on this, "Walk, Listen, Learn, Follow-up," I discuss at length in my book *Managing Difficult Employees*.]

Most managers and senior executives don't have enough contact with the people in the trenches – not nearly enough. And when they do make an effort to contact them, to acknowledge that they actually exist (And believe me this is how it feels!), they don't do it by walking around and getting to know them in their space.

Though many managers in large corporations understand this idea in principle, they don't seem to quite 'get it.' (Actually far too many don't 'get it' at all!) Having meetings, large or small, it doesn't matter the size, is not acknowledging someone. Even one-on-ones fail the test of MBWA most of the time. Luncheons, town-hall-meetings, 'give-and-takes,' none of these fulfill the real needs that people have.

It is about getting out there and talking with people. Giving them the opportunity to see and speak with you in their environment, not yours, and not in some neutral space like a town hall meeting. The manager who gets out into the factory or cubicles with his employees has a chance to really meet people, to share their experiences and work concerns with them, and to listen, really listen. He gets to see 'his people'* in their environment and that does make a big difference. Peters says it best, "...the point of being out and about...is to listen and facilitate, not give commands and inspect." (*Thriving On Chaos*) It is also not just about being seen. You can walk around a good bit and not engage or acknowledge people.

> *"Your people" – My Dad always talked about "my people." It didn't have anything to do with ownership, it had to do with caring and making a difference. "I need to get down to the bank and sign the checks for my people or they won't get paid until after the holiday."

Acknowledgment is about being willing to understand who a person is and what they mean to your team and business. It is not on some paper or evaluation and it is not about recognition, awards, or ceremony (although these are important, too. See Chapters 25, 27, 28, & 29)

It is about saying,

> "I know you are here."

> "I appreciate your efforts."

> "I am trying to pay attention to more than my administrative duties."

It is saying and meaning,

> "This business needs you"

It is really about saying:

**You are important!**

It is so simple but it SEEMS much harder because we can't find the time – because we always have more important things on our desks and on our calendars.

If you glean nothing else from this book, pay attention to this:

**There is nothing more important than acknowledging the people who work for you.**

There is nothing, ever, that should get in the way of getting out and spending time with 'your people.' Whether you are a low-level manager or a high-level executive, you need to do this as often as possible and nothing else should take precedence. If it comes down to a choice of scheduling or attending another meeting, or spending two hours walking the halls, walk the halls. It will pay many more benefits over the long haul, far more.

Acknowledging people helps motivate them to do their best.

Always keep in mind this simple truth: People NEED to be acknowledged. It is fundamental to our existence as human beings.

Here is a very important truth about work and life:

Every time I make the effort to acknowledge someone,

**I** am rewarded.

# 21. Respect

Synonyms: esteem; value; prize; honor; regard

Antonyms: disrespect; contempt; discourtesy; rudeness; disregard; put-down; demeaning

Respect other people, not because they are wrong,

or even because they are right,

but because they are human.

(John Cogley/Koob).

"The talented employee may join a company because of its charismatic leaders, its generous benefits, and its world-class training programs, but how long that employee stays and how productive he is while he is there is determined by his relationship with his immediate supervisor."

(Buckingham and Coffman)

At times, perhaps far too often, we lose sight of the important fact that there is something very fundamental that we all share. When we really think about it, even when we try hard to put our fingers on what it really is, it is never easy to describe. What makes us human? What is our humanity?

But when we do make that effort, we take a step higher on the ladder of what humanity is all about.

Every time we say something negative about someone

we are showing them disrespect.

**"But...."**

There are no buts....buts are excuses.

51

Excuses are a way of avoiding responsibility

for what we do and say.

Yes, sometimes we have to evaluate, give bad news, and generally be a manager. Leaders learn that there are always ways to say things so that they are far less damaging and much kinder. They also know that you say things directly to a person. You don't write memos, or send an e-mail, or pawn it off on someone else.

Here is a revised version of the statement above:

Every time we say something negative about someone to another

person, we are showing disrespect to both people.

AND, in essence,

we are not respecting ourselves

at this point, either.

Respect is a tenuous thing. It has a great deal to do with ego. If a person has a positive self-worth and is undeterred by others' opinions, respect is appreciated, but not necessary. Unfortunately that is rarely the case. Most of us have to deal with our egos every day and we feel bad, hurt, angry, defensive, and/or abused when we are not offered basic respect by others, by our team members, by our boss.

Difficultpeople.org is all about understanding and working with difficult people. Often difficult people have a tremendous need for appreciation, acknowledgment, and to feel respected by others, especially their peers. The irony is that because we see them as being difficult much of the time, it can be harder to give them what they need so desperately.

Respect goes beyond what we say to others. There are many subtle ways in which we 'put down' subordinates and peers. These can be very difficult to ferret out unless someone is willing to really look and to ask about them.

Consider these few examples:

> Poorly maintained, cramped working conditions, while executives have suites
>
> Dirty restrooms
>
> Bureaucracy that screams out that we don't trust people:
>
>> Forms for every little thing
>>
>> Rules guiding every decision we are 'allowed' to make
>>
>> Umpteen signatures up the chain for approval
>
> Privileges that are reserved for the few

> Impersonalness (as perceived by others)
>
> is the ultimate discourtesy.
>
> (Peters & Austin)

Good leaders are willing to ask their employees what business practices, procedures, forms, and accepted roles are demeaning or disrespectful. Employees will tell you what they feel if you are sincere about changing things. Don't ask if you are not ready to tackle their concerns and willing to make changes. You will very likely face some serious considerations.

Employees will sincerely appreciate a leader's efforts to listen to their concerns. The effort itself shows respect. Following up with issues that are raised with decisive action whenever feasible, discussing alternatives, or commiserating when brick walls are run into, means even more.

Respect can mean all the difference in the world in turning dispirited people around and in building a cohesive dynamic team.

When you respect your team members, and they know it, they can more easily develop their own personal self-respect. Then the team begins to develop a sense of unity and group respect. This is what builds solidarity and pride in an organization.

# 22. Courteous

Synonyms: polite; affable; cultivated; respectful; couth

Antonyms: discourteous; disrespectful; uncouth; slight

Being courteous with people comes with having respect for them, but it goes beyond this. We are capable of respecting all humanity and their right to be here. We can respect the differences we have with another person. We can respect their space, their needs, and their concerns. We don't necessarily have to respect certain aspects of their personality, i.e. if they are rude, boorish, overpowering, negative, whining, blaming, complaining, etc. However, we can always be courteous to them in spite of their negative behavior.

General courtesy underlies an overall respect for a person's right to be. Every way in which we work and interact with others shows who we are as human beings. Courtesy and Kindness (see Chapter 31) can go a long way to helping a difficult person be 'less difficult.'

Being courteous can be,

Making an extra effort to ask a person how they are doing.

It can be holding a door for someone.

It can be letting them have the floor in a meeting, when you would rather move ahead with another issue.

It can be listening, really listening, to them and what is important about their viewpoint, a project, or other work-place issues.

It can be getting back to them as quickly as possible because that is how you would like to be treated too.

It can be as simple as treating everyone as an equal – which, when you think about it, isn't so easy to do, especially in a work environment.

True courtesy is coupled with sincerity. Being courteous as an exercise, because you think it is the right thing to do, will quickly be seen through. Be courteous because you DO respect a person's right to feel, think, and act as they need to at this point in their life. It is who they are because of many, many factors. You can try to understand that and respond as a person who respects others' rights, or you can choose something else.


Choose wisely.

# 23. Attention

Synonyms: interest; attending; observance; regard; mindfulness; consideration

Antonyms: inattention; ignoring; disregard; snub; neglect; slight

Paying attention to others is a courtesy. Letting the members of your team and organization know they are important is often a simple matter of paying attention to who they are and what they contribute. Getting out and talking with team members in the trenches is one important means of reaching out to people who work for and with you, but it is only one tool.

Paying attention to others also means making an effort to understand what is important to them by listening carefully to what they say and how they say it. It also means weighing thousands of bits of information that allows you insight into what makes them tick, what motivates them, what helps them improve, and what is unique about them that will add to your team and organization's growth and development.

Good leaders know their people. They develop the ability to sense and understand a person's strengths, their interest areas, their weaknesses, how they interact with others, and their needs. They pay attention and use all those bits of information to give them an image of what that person is all about and how they can best contribute to the organization.

Business is not just about getting the right people on the bus; it is very much about getting the right people on the bus and in the right seats. (Jim Collins) And once they are in the right seat utilizing the best they have to offer by paying attention.

By developing this kind of understanding a leader can learn to put the right person on the right task so that they are successful and the team/project is successful. One employee might be a super sleuth at ferreting out the tiny details that can mess up a project, whereas another might be a total disaster assigned to this type of task, but will be a tremendous help in brainstorming alternatives when the project gets stuck.

Understanding bridges many communications gaps. True understanding comes not just from these types of techniques, but also from being willing to ask – being willing to ask the employee directly:

> "What type of work are you best equipped and motivated to handle?"

> "What can I and other team members do to help motivate your best performance?"

> "What do you feel you need to change/learn to contribute your best to this team?"

> "What needs to happen to make this transition work for you?"

> And so on.

It is amazing how rare it is to find leaders who are willing to ask, listen, and make an effort to understand their employees. Leaders who have the guts and foresight to ask the type of questions that help them develop insight into what is important to their employees are much more likely to be able to quickly build effective and dynamic teams.

Another very important consideration is how much attention you are paying to whom. If all of your attention is being spent on problems, concerns, and problem people, that sends a very specific message – and not a very good one. In *First Break All the Rules*, Buckingham and Coffman, state that, "'No News' Kills Behavior....Since human beings are wired to need attention of some kind, if they are not getting attention they will tend, either subconsciously or consciously, to alter their behavior until they do."

I would extend the first part of this statement by saying, "No News" Kills **Good** Behavior. AND it can help create an environment where grumbling, complaining, finger-pointing, behind-the-back tactics, etc. become the norm. People worry when they don't know what is happening. Worry creates angst, stress, and ultimately negative behaviors.

Many large companies spend a tremendous amount of money, energy, and time in developing scales, methods, forms, etc. to delineate ad infinitum various aspects of their people and jobs. While this may provide useful information for evaluation and training purposes, it rarely gets to the real need, which is to understand the cares and needs of employees – real people. And unfortunately except for once-a-year evaluation purposes, this information is rarely used at all. If these types of information gathering are a necessary part of the system, then it is a leader's job to ensure that what is gleaned from them is used in as positive and constructive a way as possible, i.e. someone needs to pay attention to it.

The leader who wants to make a difference goes beyond these formal systems and works directly with his/her personnel to understand personal motivations and needs.

Attention, as I discuss it here, has two important considerations:

> Attention given to staff and personnel because people appreciate that someone notices and cares;

> And,

> Paying attention to who they are and their needs and concerns in such a way that your understanding can help them, the team, and the organization.

Both are important to team and business success.

Both are critical to success for a leader.

# 24. Support

Synonyms: back; endorse; sustain; affirm; bolster; defend

Antonyms: negate; contradict; belie; oppose

It is our responsibility as a leader to be concerned with how our employees, coworkers, and yes, even our bosses, feel supported.

It is easy to give lip-service to the concept of supporting others; but being there for someone through thick and thin, especially during difficult times and major change, reflects our character as a leader. We all appreciate and occasionally need the support of others. When we provide it, we are more likely to receive it in return.

People know, very quickly, whether you will step up to the plate for them when push comes to shove. They will know if you have what it takes to go up against the 'higher-ups' when you feel strongly about something, when you believe changes need to be made, and/or when you need to look after someone on your team. They will know whether they are important to you by how you deal with them and others. Every decision, action, and conversation you have will be noted, recorded, and made part of their long-term memory of who you are. Things in an office get around very quickly. If you misstep in your support of your personnel, it could be a long road back.

Good leaders know when and how to approach the powers-that-be to stand up for what is right for their team and most importantly the players on their team. They also know how to deal with people in as open and as unbiased a way as possible. Honesty and openness play a major role in how team members perceive your support for them and what they are trying to accomplish. You don't always have to do things their way and you don't always have to agree with them. You do need to be up-front about what you are doing and why, and you need to provide updates and information whenever feasible so people can stay on board with the decisions that are made. You have to be willing to bring bad news gracefully, without putting it off or trying to hide it. You have to be able to show that you have considered various possibilities and that you have made an effort.

Important hint: Making an effort on their behalf is often much more important than the result, as long as they know you sincerely tried.

Support is also an attitude that comes from the leader and becomes a part of the whole team's approach. John Maxwell says it best,

"Teamwork is birthed when you concentrate on

'we' instead of 'me.'"

*(The 17 Indisputable Laws of Teamwork)*


A great leader promotes this kind of attitude through example and through recognizing those who exemplify it through effort, creativity, and productivity. Talking the talk in the sense of cooperation and community effort is critical, too. When you show it through your actions AND say it, the message is clearer:

WE are a team

and

WE succeed or fail together

When team members understand that a leader will make an effort to support them in every possible way, and that their leader emphasizes team effort and support on a regular basis, a cohesive, focused group will likely be the result. People learn and mimic the positive (as well as negative) behavior that they see and that is reinforced.

Support means doing what you say you will do.

Support means being honest with people.

Support means knowing your people and understanding their needs.

Support means caring about how people feel about something.

Support means caring about how they feel.

# 25. Grateful

Synonyms: thankful; appreciative

Antonyms: unthankful; thankless; unappreciative

Thanking people is one of the easiest and best ways to build morale. Period.

I had a difficult time choosing between 'grateful' or 'gratefulness' and 'thankful' or 'thankfulness.' Grateful is a slightly broader term that I feel fills in the gaps between how we think of appreciation (see Chapter 19 on **Appreciation**) and being thankful or saying 'thanks.'

People need to feel appreciated at work and in life. Being grateful adds a richness to our relationships with others. This can take many forms: sometimes a nod, handshake, pat on the back, flowers, or a hug (if appropriate and if you dare!) will work. Showing we are grateful is one way that we can appreciate others and what they have done for us, our team, and our organization.

When we are grateful we usually say so and 'thank you' is still the best way I know of showing gratitude. The problem is almost all of us don't do it enough. Make it a top priority starting today. Look for opportunities to tell your personnel, all the people you work with including the very top echelons of brass, that simple phrase, "Thank you," or find another way to express gratitude that feels comfortable to you.

> "Thanks, Bob, I appreciated your getting those slides to me a day early."

> "Thanks for helping Ann with that decision Jane."

> "Thanks for everything Alice. You are a gem."

> "I really appreciated your thoughts on this project Bill. I am going to keep them in mind as I rework things."

"I know we don't agree on how this should be done John, but your insights have helped me see the broader picture. Thanks."

"I just wanted to say, 'thanks.' Beth, you've meant a lot to this group."

Be sincere. You won't have to work very hard at this once you get in the habit. People do small 'great' things all the time. We just need to recognize them and get used to saying something positive to them when the opportunity presents itself. (There are lots of opportunities every day. Pay attention!) Personalize your comments whenever feasible. It is also a good idea to do it both privately and in public, if appropriate.

It is amazing how much positivity (see Lesson 98) will come from this.

The 'difficult' people at work (morale concerns, low productivity, poor attitude, etc.) will be much more likely to begin to turn their work-life around when you find ways to thank them. You don't have to be obvious or obsequious about it, but you do have to jump on the opportunities that present themselves. Difficult people tend to need more attention and support than top performers.

Nothing beats the personal touch – saying something directly to a person. However, phone calls, e-mails, memos, and brief announcements at meetings can all be used effectively as well. Get in the habit of sending out e-mails that express positive, grateful thoughts to some of your team members at the end of every day.

AND NOTHING ELSE!

In other words, don't bog down your efforts to show appreciation and gratitude with other day-to-day, business issues. This can be a great potential motivator for the next day or for the weekend. Send some of your people home with a smile.

Great leaders appreciate their people and are willing to say so. Being loud, self-centered, and charismatic may get someone a lot of attention, but it doesn't count much in the trenches.

Show gratitude whenever possible. Better yet, feel it, then the showing will take care of itself.

# 26. Recognition

Synonyms: acknowledgment; approval; credit; commendation

Antonyms: disapproval; disfavor

Recognition in the workplace is about letting others know in public that they have done well. It can be a simple 'thanks' announced at a meeting for doing a good job, or it can be something more formal and more tangible.

We like to be recognized. When we are recognized for what we have done, we appreciate the attention. It is not necessarily as fundamental a need as being appreciated or being acknowledged, but it is nice.

Recognition is also something that has to be carefully thought about and handled judiciously. Most businesses have formal recognition procedures – evaluation processes, bonuses, certificates and awards, prizes for achieving goals, etc. These typically work fairly well if they are set up to be non-biased and have specific, well-understood criteria. However, they can be very demoralizing if they are poorly designed, biased, or mishandled.

Recognition within an organization or a team can be something that becomes a regular, formal process, or it could be more informal and based on a given set of circumstances. In its most effective form it is often spontaneous and based on a specific performance or outcome.

Good leaders find or make opportunities for their team members to receive recognition. It certainly can be overdone, but individual and team recognition can help improve morale, give people a feeling of accomplishment, encourage better effort, and give people short term goals to work toward within the scope of a major project.

As an example:

If a leader is head of product development, which is a process that goes through many phases and takes a good bit of time and team-effort across matrixes and lines, he/she can improve the overall cohesion of the group by recognizing intermediate goals and extra effort. The tendency, often, in goal-directed behavior, whether team or individual, is to dig in and drive to the finish. We forget to take note and recognize people for their efforts along the way. A long project like this may have a dozen or more intermediate steps. Making the effort to recognize milestones and small wins adds both motivation and quality to the process. Recognizing the efforts of others in the diverse teams that impact your own team is also an excellent technique.

Every day, garden variety recognition can take many forms:

An announcement at the end of a phase to congratulate everyone on their efforts, plus recognition of outstanding individual efforts

Donuts at the next core team meeting to celebrate reaching an intermediate goal or getting over a bump in the road

A luncheon to celebrate the move from one stage to another [Food almost always works!]

Memos of thanks and appreciation to members throughout the process

A specific award ceremony following success of major stages

'Fun' recognition awards to keep everyone smiling

More formal recognition devised specifically for outstanding effort and accomplishment (team and individual)

Make the most of formal recognition processes developed by the team or organization

Recognize birthdays and other special occasions with a sincere and personal note or card. Better yet, stop by their cubicle or give them a brief call. Don't leave this to your administrative assistant. Do it yourself. You might be surprised at how motivating a call from a vice-president can be to a clerk in the sales department.

Smart leaders recognize the behaviors they want to see in their employees. And believe it or not this works up and down the chain:

> "Bill, my team wanted to give you a small token of our thanks for going to bat for us with the President. Most Vice Presidents wouldn't have stuck their neck out that far. Thanks!"

> Imagine his surprise when you hand him a plaque or a certificate for a free dinner.

Often it is how we deal with recognition that has the most impact. If we make a sincere effort to show people we really appreciate what they have done and the effort they have put in, recognition doesn't have to have large tangible rewards built in.

Recognizing people IS about appreciating them – in the presence of others.

It is a great tool. It is nice. But it doesn't take the place of a good down-home,

> "I really appreciate you. You are terrific. Thanks for being on my team."

Use recognition honestly, and often.

# 27. Celebration

Synonyms: festivity; jubilation

Antonyms: depreciation; disparagement

Sometimes we need to celebrate – just let everything rest for a brief period of time, remove ourselves from the stresses of work, and 'have a party.' You don't have to spend a lot of time and money. Celebrations can be small,

> A cake for some hard team effort with a few appropriate speeches

> A lunch where every one gets away from it all to enjoy each others company outside of the stresses of work

> A congratulatory letter sent to team members.

Or, they can be quite extensive,

> Team or organization-wide celebrations

> Marking a success

> Getting a huge new contract

> Reaching a major goal

> Annual celebratory events

> And so on.

Celebrations are important, but they need to be heartfelt and well-planned. A team or group picnic in the summer may be meant as a type of celebration, but unless it is AN EVENT with appropriate celebration attached, it is just another team get-together that may or may not have some team-building aspects to it.

Celebrations are all about good feelings and positive experiences. They can, and should include recognitions, awards, congratulatory speeches, and/or other forms of letting people know that there is reason to be happy and proud of what has been accomplished.

My conception of a celebration is that it is something that occurs only for special circumstances and is always the result of successes. It should almost never be an annual or regular event, though celebrations might occur as part of an annual event to recognize specific team and organizational accomplishments. Celebrations can be overdone, over-long, and too frequent.

> Note: be especially aware of the overly long celebration. It quickly becomes something far removed from people enjoying themselves. Three hours of awards, speeches, and recognition is not fun.

Help facilitate more intimate and personal celebrations as well – two or three people getting together to celebrate getting around a big hurdle in their project, etc. A wise leader encourages and facilitates small celebrations within their teams as a means of intermittent recognition of work well done.

Add some joy to your team – celebrate and enjoy your successes. It will help you get through the tough spots!


"Celebrate what is RIGHT with the world!"

(*National Geographic* documentary)

# 28. Ceremony

Synonyms: honoring; occasion; affair; observance; rite; ritual; notice

Antonyms: everyday; common; mundane; workaday; usual; unremarkable

Marking special events in life and work in a formal manner is important to building esprit-de-corps. It is critical to giving members of a team or organization a sense of belonging and ownership in the overall enterprise and in their work.

Large organizations often have a variety of ceremonies to mark special occurrences: schools celebrate graduation day; teams celebrate accomplishments; large groups like the International Olympic Committee or the United Nations have ceremonies to mark the beginnings and endings of special events, and so on. Even small groups have specific ceremonies to heighten the effect of transitions and to emphasize the special nature of belonging. A good example would be the rituals associated with entry into a fraternity or sorority.

Ceremonies can be an effective means of building a team's overall comradery. They can be a simple but poignant celebration of a specific type of accomplishment, e.g. getting a project through a certain stage; a small rite of passage associated with someone entering or leaving the group; or a special marking of someone's promotion within the department.

Unlike celebrations, which can be spontaneous, ceremonies are typically something that happen consistently and they have a certain ritual associated with them. The ritual can be more formal, for example – the ceremonies for entering an honor society; or they can be a something like a small luncheon that is set up specifically to celebrate and say goodbye to a partner moving to a new department or job.

Unfortunately except for very large and cumbersome occasions, big business has gotten away from ceremony, and smaller organizations and teams have gotten into the habit of 'maybe having something' when such and such happens.

While a leader needs to use ceremony judiciously and in moderation, it can be an effective means of bringing people together and helping them feel more a part of the group and what it is all about. It can help team members look forward to special rites of passage or successes in ways that spontaneous celebrations can't.

Ceremony helps people belong. And that can make all the difference in the world in how they work together.

# 29. Reward

Synonyms: honor; reinforce; accolade; award; laurels; prize

Antonyms: punish; penalize; penalty; ignore; snub; neglect

Rewards and awards often come with recognition, celebrations, and ceremonies. A good leader learns to use rewards intelligently as a form of encouragement and as an observance of success.

Business today seems locked into rewards as a result of evaluation processes. They are often formulaic 'doctrines' that neutralize in many ways the benefits that could be gained by honoring people for what they have accomplished. Too often these systems become accepted, mundane, little appreciated and unfortunately, often a deprecating, rather than motivating, process. Those who do well, which typically means only the few at the very top of the scale, are at best pleasantly pleased with their reward. Those in the mid to lower levels of these reward systems feel anything but grateful and rewarded. It is more typical for them to feel as if they have failed.

Wise leaders reward people because of what they accomplish – regularly.

Rewards and Awards can be simple pats on the back or congratulatory memos, tickets to a game or a coupon for a burger and fries, a special dinner, plaques, certificates, or even a day off. They don't have to be big or monetary. Often small little expressions that say 'You did a great job,' or 'I appreciate your being here,' are much more powerful and effective as a means of employee satisfaction and morale boosting than any evaluation process and financial reward – hence the emphasis in previous chapters on acknowledgement, appreciation, and recognition.

This is a key point to consider in depth. If you asked anyone which they would rather have – a thousand dollar bonus or a certificate handed out in a team meeting (because you and Suzie were the two people to exceed your sales goal this quarter) – everyone would probably take the thousand dollars. But if you could evaluate the pride, esprit, and genuine feelings associated with these rewards and the long-term individual and team benefit, the certificate would win hands down – every time!

Every time!!!!

In the same vein, evaluation systems tend to reward even average and below average performance. It is common in big business for people who get the lower rating levels to still receive financial bonuses. Yet they probably feel anything but rewarded, much less motivated by the largess because they received a poor evaluation.*
More spontaneous, accomplishment-focused rewards on a team or organizational basis show specifically where and why the award is being given.

> *The business practice, often hidden beneath layers of bureaucracy, of 'requiring' mid-level managers to create some type of hierarchical structure in evaluating their team members is often very damaging motivationally.

It is important for managers to ensure that rewards and awards do not become expected and especially to watch for bias creeping into the process.

Employee involvement in reward processes can be valuable, but spontaneous awards and recognition are equally valuable and have the added benefit of bringing a quick smile and a 'You made my day,' feeling. This is an especially useful tool during times of stress and change. When teams are working hard, dealing with tense situations, and putting in long hours, a small celebration with accompanying rewards/awards can turn the whole mood around.

Good leaders keep an ear to the ground and know when a little extra can make all the difference in the world in keeping everyone on track and motivated.

Service to others includes understanding that the people you work with ARE special and deserve to be recognized – not just as a part of some organization hoopla, but as individuals who contribute daily to your team and organization's success.

Celebrate what is right with your people and you will be celebrating more success as a result.

# PART III

# Honoring the Humanity of Others

## 30. Caring

Synonyms: concern; regard; guardianship; consideration; like; tending

Antonyms: uncaring; thoughtless; no concern; dislike; avoidance; unaffectionate

> I will stop providing you with pearls of wisdom and I will elaborate on one. The one piece of advice which I believe will contribute more to making you a better leader and commander, will provide you with greater happiness and self-esteem, and at the same time advance your career more than any other advice which I can provide you. And it doesn't call for a special personality, and it doesn't call for any certain chemistry. Any one of you can do it. And that advice is that **you must care**... (my emphasis)
>
> [Speech at the Armed Forces Staff College given by Lieutenant General Melvin Zais former commander of the 101st Airborne quoted in *A Passion for Excellence*, Peters and Austin]

Caring, at first glance, may sound too 'touchy-feely' for most managers. That is why I like this quote. When a three-star general speaks, people listen.

> My Dad was a 'Bird' (Full) Colonel in the U.S. Army having worked his way up from the ranks after being drafted in World War II. When I spoke at his funeral, I talked about one thing – Dad cared about 'his people.' He cared so much that even after retiring he spent the next twenty-five plus years supporting the soldiers at Ft. Campbell, KY, home of the 101st Airborne, in a thousand different ways. The line at my Dad's funeral lasted three

73

solid hours and that was on a Mother's Day and it was also a graduation weekend. Soldiers, guys who lived and fought in the trenches, got up and spoke about him. That is caring.

For all his idiosyncrasies and faults (he could be as stubborn as they come) Dad could enter any business establishment in Hopkinsville, KY and everyone knew him, but most importantly, when he left that business, everyone he had spoken to felt better. What a legacy to leave this earth with! If I learn anything from my dad, I hope I can eventually learn that.

Caring means liking what you do and the people you do it with. It doesn't have to be very sentimental, although it might sometimes feel that way on special occasions or if/when you or someone else moves on or retires.

Great leaders, whether they are gruff or easy-going, care about 'their people' and their work. It shows in their commitment, their passion, their integrity, how they handle responsibility, and their self-worth and self-discipline. You can always tell the ones who care only about themselves.

People who work for leaders who care will bend over backwards to do their best. No matter how tough they are, no matter what their style of leadership, there is something about a caring leader that shows through and makes all the difference in the world.

Lt. Gen. Zais goes on in his speech to talk about really listening to your men – really listening to their concerns and who they are and what is important to them.

I would encourage you to focus on thinking about and developing many of the qualities discussed in Part II: Service, of this book. Fundamentally it comes from something inside yourself that needs to be awakened.

How do you show you care about 'your people' and your work?

If you don't or can't care about 'your people' and your work – get out of the business of leadership – because while you may get rich and have power, you will be very, very lonely.

# 31. Kindness**

Synonyms: warm; human-centered; good; genial; amiable; benevolent; good-hearted; compassionate; charitable; considerate; caring

Antonyms: malevolent; unforgiving; bad-hearted; self-centered; cold; inconsiderate; unsympathetic; uncaring

> "When you have the choice between being right
>
> and being kind, choose being kind."
>
> (Wayne Dyer)

Kindness is at the root of humanity. We certainly can choose other ways to interact with people. You can treat your fellow-workers and employees 'as a boss,' 'as a manager,' or you can treat them as a leader. Leaders understand that dealing with others IS all about humanity. One of the overarching concepts at difficultpeople.org is that kindness, even in the face of incredible boorishness, rudeness, and even belligerence, works so much better than anything else. You can respond in kind – but unless the other person is being positive – it is stupid. Respond in <u>kindness</u> instead.

Being kind often accomplishes the following:

An immediate lessening of the stakes

Surprise on the part of the other person – they are often TRYING to get you to REACT and lose control

A change in the dynamics of your relationship with the other person (especially if you do this several times and they don't get the reaction they want from you)

A much better feeling after this 'episode' in your life is over – because positivity is so much better than negativity.

Kindness can make a huge difference to everyone on your team and within your purview at work.

I love the quote above by Wayne Dyer. I heard another gem from a participant in a difficultpeople.org teleclass. It was a question you can ask yourself:

"Do you want to be right or be happy?"

It is amazing how much time and effort we put into 'being right.' When we step back and really think about how important an issue is and our need to be 'right' about it, most of the time it certainly isn't worth our time, effort, and the angst we are putting ourselves and others through. It is much better to be kind.

Being right is all about ego and nothing about being kind. Next time you get into a discussion with someone, step back mentally and see whether your ego is playing a role in being right. See if you can find a way to let go of being right and seek a solution that is more kind. Many, many times it is surprising how we can find a means to be kind and not really give up anything at all in the process, but when we are wrapped up in ego we can't see anything but a very narrow path through our 'being right.'

Kindness can take many forms. The whole of Part II of this book is an essay on ways to be and show kindness to others. This can be done with a passing compliment, a kind word, a smile, a pat on the back, or if you are really daring and the person would understand, a hug. Hugs might be the ultimate expression of caring and kindness.

Just thinking about a hug brings a smile to my face!

Kindness is one of those "Do unto others...' things. It is good for them and it is good for you. When I am kind, I am in effect paying myself a big bonus. I have a better day and the extra bonus is that I may have made someone else's day, too.

What does it cost?

You might have to give up being right occasionally. You might have to give up a bit of your ego. You might even have to work at it for awhile – until it comes a bit more naturally.

What does it pay back?

Good feelings a thousand-fold in return, and often kindness 'back-at-cha.'

Make kindness more than a habit. Make it a part of who you are. It takes self-worth (Chapter 42) and Self-awareness (Chapter 40). It takes being human.

**Are you brave enough?**

# 32. Empathy

Synonyms: understanding; insight; intuitive; sympathize; perceptiveness; compassionate

Antonyms: unsympathetic; unperceptive; uncompassionate

Empathy: The projection of one's own personality into the personality of another in order to understand him better; ability to share another's emotions or feelings (Webster's, New World Dictionary)

> "Leadership is all about understanding players."
>
> (Maxwell, *The 17 Indisputable Laws...*)

Having a sense of what someone is feeling and thinking is a vital quality found in many good leaders. It goes beyond evaluations and listening, to tuning in to subtle aspects of your interactions with other people. It takes self-awareness (see Chapter 40) and paying attention to others (Chapter 41). It also has a great deal to do with caring and kindness.

Empathy is not about using personal information and clues to get what you want or to use that as leverage against another person; it is about supporting and helping others.

An empathetic leader has a good feel for the undercurrents of emotions that ebb and flow within a team and/or organization. He/she uses this understanding to make adjustments, ease stresses, and to find ways to appreciate and recognize people when they need a boost, etc.

We often associate empathy with women, however, all human beings have the capacity to empathize with others. It may seem like a magical or inborn quality if you don't have it naturally. However, it can be developed and practiced. One needs to learn how to observe oneself first and foremost, and to pay attention to others, too – what they say, how they say it; how they react to others and events; and how they interact with others.

Most people sincerely appreciate the effort a person makes to understand what is important to them. Your effort is a form of acknowledgment and recognition.

When a leader is tuned in to these subtle nuances that permeate and affect our work every day, he is much more likely to be able to make adjustments that help support personnel through difficult times. Taking this knowledge and simply talking about issues with others can make a huge difference in how people feel and the overall tenor of the workforce. Ignoring them creates a vacuum in which things can quickly escalate.

Pay attention on a deeper level to what is happening with your team personnel. You will be a better leader and person as a result.

# 33. Compassion

Synonyms: caring; sympathy; kindness; concern

Antonyms: unconcern; indifference

Kindness and compassion are inexorably linked in my mind. When I speak about kindness in my seminars I always link it to compassion. Kindness is active; it is something we do. Compassion is a feeling and attitude that often precipitates our acts of kindness.

Compassion takes empathy to another level. I believe we can empathize in a way with others, but not necessarily feel real compassion for them.

Compassion means I care about 'my people,' as my dad liked to say.

Our compassion for others doesn't have to be overly sentimental. It means we do care about what happens to them, how they are getting along, how they feel at their job and even concern for how things are going for them in general. It also means that we wish them the best in developing their potential, reaching their personal goals, and making the most of their time on our team.

Being compassionate is not difficult if we are in touch with our humanity. It is not difficult when we are dealing with excellent, above average, and even average personnel. Where compassion can be hard to feel is when we are dealing with difficult personalities, poor performing individuals, and/or people with negative attitudes.

Caring, kindness, empathy, and compassion take on a whole new perspective when the situation is less than ideal. Difficult people present us with unique challenges to our own self-worth. Understanding and supporting all your people means you have to have a firm belief in who you are and what you are about. A truly compassionate leader is someone who has a deep understanding of his own needs, wants, and desires, and who can project his own positive self-worth to others.

Compassion is about feeling. If we can't be sensitive to ourselves and our own emotions, we won't be very successful in understanding and helping others.

Be open to caring for yourself first and foremost; then you will be open to others.


"Compassion is Kindness in the most difficult of circumstances."

(Koob)

# 34. Patience

Synonyms: forbearance; tolerant; composure; endurance; sufferance; self-control

Antonyms: impatience; nervousness; restlessness; fretfulness

Patience has a great deal to do with how we perceive the world. Our interpretation of events and interactions affects what we are willing or not willing to tolerate. I can be quite patient when I am doing something I like, like sitting in a tree stand with my bow waiting for a buck to walk by. However, I may be very impatient when I am wading through layers of a phone system to finally reach and actually talk to a customer representative who, unfortunately far too often, has no clue as to how to solve my concern anyway.

I have known some very patient people who get very impatient when something or someone tweaks one of their hot buttons. Organized people can be very impatient with unorganized people. 'Get it done' people can easily get frustrated with 'get it right people,' and vice-versa. Non-hunters can be very intolerant and hence impatient with hunters. And so on.

When we can step back and realize that our differences as people, especially differences in how the way we look at things affects our ability to be patient, we have made a major leap in learning. When we become more tolerant of things that don't quite go the way we want them to, or people who don't act the way we think they should, we have become much more patient (and kind).

Patience, fundamentally, is **self-control** (see Chapter 8).

Trying to control others is how and why many people have difficulties with patience. I would like to control the 'difficulties' of a phone system or the incompetence of the person on the other end of the line, but what is the likelihood of my succeeding? Is it worth all the frustration I build up in myself in dealing with this by being impatient, not in control? The truth is I can only control myself.

When we look closely at the circumstances surrounding our impatience, control issues won't be far removed.

> As I work on my own tendency to be impatient, it is almost amusing to watch myself when I lose the battle. Invariably, however, when I make the effort, I learn about myself in the process. Over time I am learning what makes me tick, what makes others tick, and how to better control my reactions and to hopefully learn more patience.

Good leaders know that being patient, especially in difficult situations or with difficult people, can pay huge dividends. Maintaining one's cool in the face of difficulties sends a very strong message to others about who you are, what is important, and what is acceptable within your sphere of influence. When we really think about it, everything we do and say in the workplace sends very loud and clear messages to our personnel.

**When it comes to patience – what message are you sending?**

# 35. Generous

Synonyms: charitable; benevolent; unselfish; giving; freehearted; liberal; openhanded; munificent; magnanimous

Antonyms: stingy; uncharitable; selfish; cheap; chintzy; tight-fisted; parsimonious, penurious

The best leaders I have known are the ones who will bend over backwards if it will help support a colleague or employee. Whether it is offering assistance, encouragement, mentoring/ coaching, training, or just a shoulder to lean on, they are there... and their employees know it.

I have known competent managers who knew nothing of generosity.

I have worked for skilled technicians, great organizers, brilliant intellectuals, and outgoing bombasts. Only a very few of these knew what being selfless and magnanimous meant.

True generosity comes from the heart and has much to do with the first five terms in this section: caring, kindness, empathy, compassion, and patience.

> To be generous one must care. It is not so much about 'handouts' as it is about extending your hand to help.

> Generous people are kindhearted. It is kindness that expects no return beyond the simple act of reaching out.

> To be truly generous one must be able to empathize with others. It is how you can know how to help.

> Generosity is often the result of compassion for others. It is a deep-seated desire to help others who are in need.

> It takes patience to be generous to all. Patience with our self, patience with the world and what it manages to stir up on a daily basis, and patience with the trials and tribulations of others.

**It is not something you do; it must come from the heart.**

# 36. Responsive

Synonyms: sensitive; aware; tractable; reactive; susceptible

Antonyms: insensitive; unresponsive; unaware; intractable

An interesting technique of managers and leaders that seems to be gaining more and more momentum in today's business climate is the non-responsive reaction to events, queries, suggestions, and the like. It is a technique that can be very effective if used in a judicious manner, but unfortunately it tends to be far too prevalent in the business world and much over-used by some managers.

A leader can use this technique to draw out ideas from an employee. As an example: if I go in to my boss with several questions about how to deal with various aspects of my budget, or perhaps help with the evaluation of my employees, instead of answering directly, she might counter with, "Tell me what you think is the best course of action." This and similar responses can be used to promote the development of leadership qualities like creative thinking, analysis of a problem, finding a strategy, etc. However, if this is the predominant technique the manager is using with her employees, they may feel they are out in deep left field with no one to go to for help, support, or advice.

A president of an organization I once worked for had what I considered to be the very bad habit of completely ignoring any request, project, idea, or endeavor he didn't like. There was never any response. The 'requestee' was literally left hanging forever, not knowing whether any action was being considered or taken. In many other ways this leader had many good qualities, but this non-response quality was extremely frustrating. After a manager was there for awhile they became inured to this 'system' but it was never very comfortable.

A good leader knows when and how to balance being responsive to concerns and ideas of employees and when to give them more space to grow on their own. It can be a fine line.

Most people far prefer to know something, even if it is negative, than to have no response at all. Leaders need to be sensitive to personnel concerns and needs and be responsive to them.

Timeliness is a major aspect of responsiveness. Tabling something indefinitely can be more demoralizing than a quick, "No, I don't like this." I was at a leadership seminar and one of the pieces of advice they gave us was to make sure we only handled a piece of paperwork once. That, as it turned out, was virtually impossible to fully implement as a middle manager, but it always stuck with me. Now, whenever feasible, I try to get things responded to as quickly as possible. People appreciate it and it is amazing how your workload seems to decrease if you keep this idea in mind and implement it at every possible turn.

Good managers find ways to respond quickly. They learn to take notes, keep reminders, organize their schedule, and make time for the important things – like getting back to someone.

Responsive takes on a slightly different meaning in the Boy Scout motto, "Be Prepared." This is one of those little sayings that sticks with you throughout life. We have the capability of responding much more effectively and quickly if we have a handle on things and have all our ducks in a row.

Today I see far too many managers and business leaders coming to meetings unprepared. Then they wonder why so much time is wasted. If everyone had reviewed the charts, slide decks, and memos prior to the meeting it could have easily been half as long and far less stressful for the presenter and everyone else in the room, too. Again, leaders set the stage for what everyone else does by example. If they come unprepared, guess what message that sends?

Make sure you are prepared, and expect everyone else to be prepared. Otherwise you are wasting 'my' time. And guess what? I don't like to waste time.

# 37. Grace

Synonyms: elegance; poise; assuredness; beauty; blessing; adorn; ornament

Antonyms: inelegant; undignified

Grace: "elegance and beauty of movement and expression" (http://www.synonym.com)

Grace is not often associated with leadership. It is not a term that even necessarily needs to be on this list, because there certainly have been great leaders who haven't had it. However it strikes me as one of those small things that we notice about someone, and not just in women. It is something that sets a person slightly apart from their fellows – something that we remember about them long after we have left their presence. (Lundin and Peters both talk about Grace in their works)

I haven't met any of the great leaders of the world, but a few who strike me as having had a certain style, a bit or more of grace are: Queen Elizabeth II, Gandhi, J. F. Kennedy; the Dalai Lama; Robert E. Lee; and Mother Theresa. Just thinking about various leaders brings up two thoughts: "Who else could make this list from great leaders of the past and present?" and, "What is it about them that says, 'they have grace'?"

Grace is one of those terms that is hard to define, though the definition above was as close as I could come. I think it is even harder to pinpoint exactly what makes a person grace-ful. It is an attitude in a sense, a style perhaps, a way of carrying oneself, but it is more than that, too.

It may have something to do with kindness, courteousness, appreciation, empathy, patience, and certainly self-confidence and self-worth. But these terms don't really define it either.

The point I think I am trying to make here is that when one has this quality about them, it adds to their affect and their effect as a leader. It is not so much something that we work on, but that we can think about. Trying to be 'poised' or 'elegant' or striving for an "elegance and beauty of movement and expression" would likely be awkward, just a bit silly, and relatively fruitless unless one was bound for a finishing school for debutantes.

It is a rare quality. I think it does have a great deal to do with how we feel about ourselves and how we feel and care about others. It is included here because just thinking about it may have some value for leaders. It is one of those extras that makes a great leader different and pleasurable to be around.

# PART IV
# Perception

## 38. Self-awareness**

Synonyms: self-cognizance; knowingness; knowing oneself;

Antonyms: ignorance; clueless

Self-awareness is the single most important key to being a successful leader. It is the foundation for building one's self-worth (see Chapter 43) self-confidence (Chapter 45) and one's identity (Chapter 47). To know yourself is to be able to control yourself in and through all of the incredible responsibilities you have, through the stresses that threaten to overwhelm you seemingly at every turn, and in your interactions with others.

Unfortunately, self-awareness is often something we take for granted. It is an area that managers tend to ignore in their own training and their own daily activities, and in their interactions with others. It is one of the primary reasons we have difficulties with others. I think it should be a required course in every business school in the country. Heck, it should be a course in every high school and university in the country – with advanced training available at college!

**"Know thyself!"**

It is the most important key to leading others well.

Linda Dominguez suggests that there is no way to improve relationships with difficult others, including your boss, without a strong sense of self-awareness (*How to Shine at Work*).

Self-awareness is also one of 'The Seven Keys' to working with difficult people at difficultpeople.org. In our online literature there is a tremendous amount written about and related to this concept. It is one of the highlighted concepts in my book, "A Perfect Day: Guide for a Better Life." There are two words I consistently use to help focus on this: **pay attention**.

> Pay attention to what you do.

> Pay attention to how you do it.

> Pay attention to what you say.

> Really pay attention to HOW you say it.

> Pay attention to your interactions with others.

> Pay attention to your reactions and responses to a host of things: situations, stresses, other people, daily activities, etc.

It takes practice to be self-aware. It takes a life-time of paying attention to truly know ourselves. In the meantime we have the opportunity to keep learning. The better we know ourselves, the easier it will be to empathize, care for, appreciate, recognize, and respect others. The more we are cognizant of who we are and how we interact with the rest of the world the more 'in integrity' we will be, the more others will trust us. The better we know our self, the more ownership we will have of our life and work.

Practicing paying attention to what we do and say and how we react and respond can become a habit fairly quickly. I think all great leaders have developed this habit to a fine degree. It shows in their work and in their interactions with others.

Self-awareness leads to a broader conception of awareness that includes our paying attention to others and to what is happening around us (see next Chapter). Practicing paying attention to yourself doesn't lead to self-centeredness, it leads to greater awareness. Self-centeredness is about everything revolving around you. A person who is self-aware understands how far from reality egotism is.

This book focuses on this very idea – the more we know ourselves, our strengths and weakness; the more we can improve who we are and how we do things and the better leader we will be.

Self-awareness also has to do with appreciation. The more aware I am of my life and work, the more capacity I have to enjoy it and to make the most of it. Here is a wonderful short poem from Matthew Arnold:

Is it so small a thing,

> To have enjoyed the sun,
>
> To have lived light in the spring,
>
> To have loved,
>
> To have thought
>
> To have done?

Sometimes I imagine how strange it would be not to "enjoy the sun, live light in the spring, love," breathe...etc.

I also think that far too often we press so hard to get to 'some-place' or to achieve some 'goal' that we forget to enjoy the process of accomplishing what we are heading toward – pay attention to getting there. You will have a lot more fun!

Most of our lives are spent getting someplace: plans, goals, places, etc. If you really want to enjoy your life, pay attention to getting to all those places you are in such a hurry to get to (or not, as the case might be). Enjoy the ride!

Even when we are facing difficulties and changes in life, we can still take time to enjoy the process. Our life is NOW; we truly do not know what tomorrow will bring. We really don't even know what the next minute will necessarily bring.

Enjoy today and those many moments you have for the rest of your life.

When you pay attention, you will.


**Self-awareness** is one of "The Seven Keys to Understanding and Working with Difficult People."

# 39. Awareness

Synonyms: cognizance; knowing; perception; sensing

Antonyms: ignorance, clueless

Pay attention to others. It shows appreciation and respect, and it helps you keep your ear to the ground so you know what is important to them and so you know when concerns arise within your group. When you pay attention to your people, they will be much more willing to open up and work with you to solve critical problems when they arise.

When we pay attention to ourselves we also pay more attention to others. It is a skill and a habit that we can develop. If I watch my own emotions and reactions, how I say and do things, and how my interactions with others go, I am already in a heightened state of awareness. It is only a slight shift in focus that helps us improve this technique in relationship to our interactions with other people and with the world and all its doings.

One technique that is especially important for leaders is developing the skill to truly listen to another person. Part of that is observing how what we say and do affects another, i.e. watching their reactions, verbal and non-verbal, to what we are doing.

> "How we think our statements affect another may be vastly different from how they do affect them, what they actually think and feel." (difficultpeople.org)

One of the hardest interpersonal techniques to learn is paying attention to how what we do and say affects another person. I often find that not only does what another person says to me affect me differently from what they intended, but that unless I pay attention, I can affect others in ways I didn't mean as well.

Until we open up our eyes and heart to this we are limiting our ability to understand others and to communicate with them as effectively as possible. People see things differently – period! And we can never tell how something impacts another person unless we pay attention to them.

We all carry a lot of 'stuff' from the past around with us, and our stuff and their stuff definitely makes a difference in how we interact.

Paying attention to ourselves and others can help ease many difficult situations.

Leaders pay attention to their people because it brings understanding, it shows concern, it is courteous, and because they learn. They learn a lot. They don't do it to manipulate, to have fuel for evaluations, or to achieve power over someone else. By paying attention over the long haul, a leader can develop a good sense of the ebb and flow of their organization. It is a much more effective means of knowing the pulse of your group than evaluations, memos, meetings, or even get-togethers.

People can tell that you have stepped up your interpersonal skills. They know when you are genuinely interested and concerned about how what you say and do impacts them.

When we pay attention to ourselves and others, we gain one other thing that is a key element to leadership – we gain the ability to control ourselves. (Chapter 8) Observing ourselves and others is in a sense like taking an instantaneous step back in our minds so that we have the opportunity to choose our response to a situation rather than reacting. Bullies, exploders, whiners and complainers, and negative people in general, all react to life around them, to what others say and do. They don't take time to consider how they impact other people. People who try to control other people, i.e. less than ideal managers and leaders, are focused outward on what everyone else is doing and saying, not inward on what impact they are making and how others are taking it.

Unfortunately, paying attention to ourselves on the surface sounds egotistical, but it is all a matter of perspective. It is how we use the tools of self-awareness and awareness of others that makes all the difference. If you have integrity (Part I of this book) and are focused on service (Part II) to others, then these are invaluable tools that can add tremendously to your skills as a leader. They also can add a great deal to how others perceive you as a leader.

Lead through kindness and honesty.

Lead as someone who can be trusted.

Lead by paying attention to your team members.

They will appreciate it and so will you.

# 40. Visibility

Synonyms: conspicuousness; obvious; 'there;' available

Antonyms: invisibility; inconspicuous; unavailable; nowhere-to-be-seen

> "Personal leadership is about visibility."
> "Personal leadership is about communication, openness,
> and a willingness to speak often and honestly,
> and with respect for the intelligence of the reader or listener."
>
> (Lou Gerstner, Jr.)

Visibility is about getting out and spending time in the trenches. [see Chapter 23] It is also more than that. A leader needs to be visible in many ways and he/she must communicate their work values and the key leadership qualities they espouse at every opportunity.

Every time you meet with, talk to, write to members of your team either individually or as a group is an opportunity to let them know what is important. (See Peters and Austin, *A Passion for Excellence,* pp. 276-277)

Too often managers assume that their colleagues and employees understand the importance of Quality, Integrity, Courtesy, etc. IF it is important to you, your team, and its goals and strategies, it needs to be out there. You need to talk about it as well as live it.

If you are quality, talk quality. Make it an integral part of speeches, memos, and even casual, 'stop by,' meetings. Say it,

> "Bob, I am glad you are on top of this memo I sent. It shows you understand what quality means to this group."

"Shawna, that is a top-notch presentation. Everyone please note the attention to detail and quality of Shawna's slide deck."

"Don, your research is great, but the report is lacking because you don't bring the most important data forward. Remember that no one will understand the quality of your work unless you bring it out."

"Don't forget everyone, that this team is all about quality. Keep up the good work."

You also have to show how important something is by representing it in your own work and interactions with others. If 'Integrity' is an essential part of who you are, then always 'be in' integrity in your work with others.

Take the top two or three values or qualities you admire and make an effort this week to talk about them whenever feasible. Your effort to focus on these even for a brief period of time will help others understand their importance and bring a new understanding and focus to your group as well as to your own personal efforts. You will likely raise your own awareness and hence efforts in these key areas as a result. Paying attention to something or someone has amazing benefits.

Visibility is also about being there for your team. Sitting in your office all day answering memos and phone calls is not very personal. Besides getting up and walking about, leaders need to make opportunities for team members to access them throughout the week. Open door time is a great idea, but plan to be there as scheduled and be willing to put down whatever you are doing to focus on whoever comes in. You can set the tone for these types of meetings by your own openness, focus, and emphasis. Brown-nosers might want to monopolize your time to start with, but not when you keep bringing them back to reality – whatever is important to you and your team, and their success, i.e. quality, solution- focused, honesty, etc.

Another good idea is a regular town hall meeting with small to medium-sized groups [Some large businesses do this with auditorium-filled meetings. This may serve a purpose, but it lacks intimacy and openness for everyone.] If you set this up as a no-holds-barred, everyone gets a chance to say what is on their mind without penalty forum, you can get to the root of discontent, concerns, and frustrations very quickly.

Food is a great catalyst for conversation – open and relaxed conversation. Invite one or more people to lunch, or have an informal get together. This can be open-ended or focus it on something the group chooses or is interested in. This could be a value, a group concern, a brain-storming session, or anything related to the individual's or group's efforts.

Visibility is not about showing off. It may be about showing another person's efforts off, or the team's efforts off, but it should never be just focused on you, and what you have done or plan to do. Good leaders use their time with employees as a time for their players to ask questions and discuss issues that are important to them and the team. Good leaders listen, facilitate, encourage, and support during these times.

> Be visible because it is good for your team, your business, and for you.

> Be visible because it is the most significant way a leader can support and motivate his/her team.

> Be visible because it matters... a lot.

# 41. Connecting

Synonyms: engaging; engagement; join; bring together; relate; link; tie; unite

Antonyms: disjunctive; disconnecting; separate; divide; disengage; detach

A leader can be visible, but not connect with people. Connecting takes visibility to another level. Just showing up or being somewhere with others doesn't mean you are engaging others. It is tough in today's business climate to spend time and effort connecting with people when everyone is over-booked and overworked. We use every free moment to 'get things done, i.e. doing e-mails or reading memos during meetings, answering phone calls while we are in one-on-ones or other meetings, reading papers or writing during presentations, doing 'walk-a-bouts' but wishing you were doing something else, etc. The problem is we are not focused on people, we are focused on everything but.

Connecting with people isn't easy from a time management standpoint. But it is critical! (see Chapter 68, Engagement) It is so critical that it should be a top priority. That is TOP PRIORITY! Not something that gets relegated to "I'll get to it next week," or "Maybe I'll squeeze it in a day or two from now." If you have to, cancel some meetings, say 'No' a few times to other meetings that crop up, or eliminate some other things you 'have to' do. Make some changes so this IS something that happens weekly/daily. Yes, it is THAT important.

Leaders must make choices. Sometimes if we are in a boring meeting or what we feel is a 'forced exercise in futility' required by someone who thinks this would be good for us, we can make a choice to spend that time constructively or not. We can choose to become engaged in or connected to what is happening. and making it something worthwhile, rather than being only half there and wasting our precious time.

I have never been in a situation in which I couldn't learn something, and when I made the effort to refocus my attention on finding out what I or my team could gain from this activity or presentation, it made all the difference in the world. Almost everything we do or are involved with has the potential to be beneficial if we make the effort to connect with it. Every person we interact with and every interaction we have with others can teach us something and be of benefit to all of us – we have to make the effort.

Connecting and engagement are active concepts. When we DO make an effort, it changes the whole dynamics of the scenario. It changes for us and for everyone else in the room. It is amazing to watch how the engagement of one or two people who connect with what a presenter is saying can change the whole group's perspective.

It works the same way with individuals. If we connect with someone by paying close attention to what is important to them, through careful listening and observing, they often will blossom and become a 'new' person. They will become more productive, more involved, and more of a team player as a result. This is a great thing to think about when dealing with difficult people. Sometimes all they want and need is to be truly engaged by someone, so they feel a part of a team and appreciated for who they are and what they can contribute.

Another way to connect with people is to find ways to get them involved. Use their strengths, build on their interests, and when you are with them, draw them out by focusing on these key areas. When they feel engaged by you, they are much more likely to step up to the plate and deal with other issues important to the team's success.

Connecting has a lot to do with caring, supporting, and really listening. Fundamentally it has to do with paying attention. Here is the best way I have seen this idea expressed: "Make the person you are with feel like the most important person in the world." (Rewritten statement of Marty Fletcher, former player and asst. coach, Quoted by Maxwell, *The 17 Indisputable Laws of Teamwork*, p. 245)

# 42. Modeling

Synonyms: represent; reproduction; archetypal; example; paradigm; exemplar

Antonyms: avoidance; evasive; dodging

Leaders need to model the behaviors they wish to see in their team members. If honesty is an important value, a leader can do nothing less than be open and honest with his compatriots and employees. It cannot be a matter of who you are with, how they are as a person or what their values are, or even the circumstances. It has to start with you.

The real key to this concept is that we model our own values every minute of every day. Whether we are directing a meeting, talking with someone one-on-one, answering a phone call, or just walking down the hall, if we say we are about quality, but let someone's less than perfect report get through the mix, that sends a much clearer message than what we are talking about. If we claim to respect others and believe everyone should be treated with courtesy, but we explode and yell when things get out-of-hand, we are expressing a completely different person than our ideal.

Our voices (volume, tone), how we carry ourselves, our focus, and our non-verbal cues all speak volumes to others, much more than our words do. We are, whether we wish to be or not, a model for our employees. They notice!

What we spend our time on is a clear signal to everyone what is important to us. Take a week and analyze in detail where you are spending the most time and effort. Look at your schedule and delineate exactly how each meeting, etc., fits your priorities. If you are spending most of your time on things other than what relates directly to your vision, your top strategies, your most important values, and your people, you are sending some other message.

When I coach managers, senior directors, and CEO's one of the first questions I ask is "What are your priorities?" Then I follow this up quickly with, "How much time are you spending on these?"

A good example is the time managers actually spend getting out and being with their people. Most managers will say this is a top priority (if they don't, I try to get them to see why it should be!). Unfortunately very few of them actually do ANY of this in the course of a week.

What exactly are you modeling?

What messages do you send your team every day?

You can only get these answers by self-observation and inquiry, i.e. don't be afraid to ask a close associate. Find out the answers, because this is exactly who you are to everyone else regardless of who you think you are!

# PART V
# Self-Value

## 43. Self-worth**

Synonyms: self-esteem; confidence; self-respect

Antonyms: self-doubt; insecurity; uncertainty

> "If you don't like yourself, you can't like other people."
>
> (Robert Heinlein)

Self-worth is how we truly feel about ourselves. It is a product of our complete past and it influences every moment of every day we are on this earth. When I react to someone else defensively, regardless of whether they are right or wrong, my reaction is the direct result of how I feel about myself.

Someone who has a strong positive self-worth deals with negativity, difficulties, concerns, and even difficult people from a solid foundation. They can choose their responses to others rather than react with little self-control because of past wrongs and deeply buried feelings. Self-awareness (see Chapter 38) and awareness of others (Chapter 39) are emphasized over and over again in my writings because I believe it is the key to working our way out of the stuff that affects us from the past to a position of positive self-worth.

> "No one can make you feel inferior without your consent."
>
> (Eleanor Roosevelt)

Sometimes it is amazing how much a person's words can hurt us. Most of us tend to carry a good bit of 'stuff' around from our past and when someone else touches on that stuff – there goes our self-worth.

Understanding ourselves by watching carefully how we react to things is one way to build our own self-worth and dispose of some of that negativity from the past. It does take time, but it is amazing what we can learn about ourselves and others in the process. Getting rid of that 'stuff' helps make life much more enjoyable, so it is well worth the effort.

Awareness of self and others also helps you avoid creating or triggering stuff in others because your positivity is showing through. It is worth thinking about!

"There is something in each of us that wants us to be Unhappy.

It creates in our imagination problems that don't yet exist...

It exaggerates problems that are already there.

It reinforces our low self-esteem..."

(The "Eeyore Effect" from *The Te of Piglet*, Hoff)

**It is our ego!**

Defensiveness is a pretty good sign that our ego is in play and our self-worth is slipping.

"Eeyores are afraid –

afraid to risk positive emotional expression, positive action,

positive involvement in anything beyond Ego."

Understanding how self-worth is different from ego is one of life's long studies. Ego is our negative replacement for our self-worth. I am beginning to believe that all the negative affect we conjure up in ourselves is the result of our ego, i.e. blaming, complaining, defensiveness, judging, worrying, and so on.

How often do we suffer from our own Eeyore Effect?

How often are we creating our unhappiness?

Here is a hint: much more often than we think.

"When we blame our unhappiness on others, it renders us powerless, because in essence, we are saying that our happiness is dependent upon the actions or approval of others. That means it is not under our control. When we stop blaming others and start taking responsibility, we take back control and power over our own happiness." (Lunden)

[Also, see **Self-control**, Chapter 8 and **Ownership** Chapter 4]

Self-worth involves self-control – true control of who we want to be. It is reaching to the roots of our being and discovering the truth of our greatness as a human being and then working to bring that to the surface every moment we can. I believe that somewhere each of us has an image of the person we want to be, in effect our ideal. This is where our self-worth must start from. When we let our ego rule we are effectively giving control over to the past and saying, "I am worthless," "I am not good enough," "I have made too many mistakes to be redeemed." Begin your road back to self-worth by touching base with your ideal you.

The truth is our life starts NOW! Everything in the past is past and we can choose to let it beat us down (our ego) or we can choose something else, i.e. letting ourselves be driven by our true self from which we can derive our positive self-worth. Even when events or people from the past impact us, we still have choices we can make: to despair and let that drive us downward, or to begin to move our life ahead. From this moment on my life can be a 'do over.' (From the movie *City Slickers*, Underwood)

I have had a million 'do-overs' in my life already. Every time I have been beaten down or beaten myself down, I have decided to move on. Each time I pick myself back up after a setback, whether major or minor, I am trying again to get it right, to make my life what I truly want it to be. If I pay attention, each one of these life episodes allows me to learn, be stronger, grow in confidence, and to value myself a bit more.

Valuing the truth about who we want to be is not ego. It doesn't raise us above other people, it raises us "...above the partialities and futilities of uninformed desire, and to rule one's self." (Spinoza/Durant)

**Self-Worth** is one of "The Seven Keys to Understanding and Working with Difficult People."

# 44. Self-respect

Synonyms: self-esteem; pride

Antonyms: unconfident; insecure; self-contempt

Self-respect is a result of our feelings of self-worth. Self-respect does have a great deal to do with how we currently look at ourselves based on our past actions and reactions. When we feel bad about something we have done, we lack in self respect. It is a very hard thing to regain unless we change how we look at ourselves.

I believe there are few people on this earth who would not wish to change a great many things about the choices they have made in the past. We all have things we feel bad about. I can conjure up several in a moment's time and I still feel chagrin at what I did. My choice is always whether to let this burden me now or to learn from it and move on, not letting it impact my self-worth.

**The key is to know yourself – the true you.**

Maybe I am an idealist, but I believe that somewhere deep within each human being is the essence of our humanity, our ideal self, how we wish we could be. I discussed an exercise related to finding out the fundamental values and qualities we aspire to in Chapter I, "Integrity." If you have completed this exercise, this would be a good time to review your short list of qualities and values and make changes if you want to. If you haven't completed this short exercise, this would be a great time to consider doing so.

Here is my 'short list.'

> Service to Others
>
> Caring, Kind and Loving
>
> Responsible for my own life and actions

Respect and Compassion for fellow men and women

Respect for all life and people's spirituality

Open and Honest

Self-aware and Self-confident

A love and joy of life

Love of learning and creativity

Other questions remain,

How can we teach this?

How can we exemplify these qualities and values in our work and life?

How do we learn to bring these to the fore in our life?

How can we learn self-respect in spite of our past?

The key to answering these questions lies in what we do from this point on with our lives:

**Anything we do to and with ourselves and to and with others**

**that doesn't foster ALL the things on our list**

**shouldn't be a part of our <u>new</u> life.**

We may not respect things about ourselves that we have done in the past. But **we can respect who we are, and who we are striving to be.** We will very likely make more mistakes. We will make poor choices and occasionally stray a bit from our values. But when we treat each as a learning experience and get back up off the ground and renew our personal commitment to our <u>self</u>, we can still respect our efforts.

Great leaders know what they value. They understand their weaknesses and foibles but they always strive to be the best they can be.

"The capacity for getting along with our neighbor depends to a large extent on the capacity for getting along with ourselves. The self-respecting individual will try to be as tolerant of his neighbor's shortcomings as he is of his own. Self-righteousness is a manifestation of self-contempt." (Hoffer, *The Ordeal of Change*)

Respecting others and the struggles they are going through is a big part of self-respect, too. When we understand ourselves and the efforts we are making, it is much easier to understand and respect the struggles of others.

They are doing the best they can for this moment in time in their lives.

Try keeping this thought in mind in every interaction you have with others. It will help you be a better leader and a kinder person.

# 45. Self-confidence**

Synonyms: assurance; poise; self-possession

Antonyms: insecurity; uncertainty

> "Arrogance is self-important, inflated, and disrespectful.
>
> Confidence is quiet and strong."
>
> (Dominguez, *How to Shine At Work*)

The self-confident leader does not have to beat down others, lord it over others at meetings, or monopolize conversations. Self-confident leaders usually listen more, ask questions, support and reward others' ideas, and keep themselves in the background (see Chapter 16, **Humility**)

I really like Linda Dominguez's quote above. **Quiet** and **Strong** are great descriptors of the best leaders I have known and read about.

> Some time ago I was at a dinner with ten executives from a major corporation. One of the attendees was a senior vice-president and the rest of the group were senior directors, directors, lower-level vice-presidents and associate directors. The senior vice-president totally dominated the conversation. No one could get much of a word in edgewise. When they did manage to say anything, he always had something to say about it that was more important. He was overpowering, bombastic, full of himself, and, I would hazard a guess, very insecure.

**Secure people do not have to place themselves above others.**

Self-confidence comes from knowing your strengths and your weaknesses.

> I used to think very little of my intellectual abilities in spite of doing straight 'A' work in graduate school and breezing through qualifying exams, etc. At that time a coach I was working with asked me why I didn't believe in myself intellectually when everyone else did, including all my professors. I told her "I don't feel very smart; I do well because I work harder than everyone else." The truth was, that when I took a closer look at myself I realized that I had abilities I didn't give myself credit for because I had accepted what others had said about me in the distant past and never let that perspective go.
>
> Today I believe in myself much more than before. I also try to understand where I have weaknesses. Whenever possible I get help from others when I realize I am over my head in any given area.

Good leaders build on their strengths and the strengths of others. They recognize their own deficiencies and complement them with people who have strengths in areas in which they are lacking. They are confident about both, because they have a handle on who they truly are. Self-confidence also allows a leader to believe in others because it helps him support and assist them in working with their strengths and weaknesses too.

**\*\*Self-Confidence** is one of "The Seven Keys to Understanding and Working with Difficult People."

# 46. Character

Synonyms: temperament; personality; disposition; moral fiber; integrity; pride

Antonyms: corrupt; immoral; dishonest; crooked

"She has character."

"He's a character."

Two different meanings – both are fairly nebulous.

What is character?

Is it something we learn?

Is it something we are born with?

Can we get some if we don't have any?

Is it just another word for integrity?

Character reflects who we are inside. Because it is what we show the world, it is what others perceive us to be. It is in a sense, the combination of all those attributes, qualities, and values that a person possesses. To have great character one could say, "She lives the 99 qualities found in this book."

Great leaders have character. It isn't always the same. Everyone's is slightly different. It does have to do with integrity, moral fiber, personality, and temperament.

Of all the terms in this book, I don't believe that it is something we specifically can work for, achieve, or change about ourselves. I think it comes as a result of our working on all the other key ideas, values, and qualities that we find important. Specifically it has to do with the other words in this section: self-worth, self-respect, self-confidence, and identity. It has something to do with how we approach life, how we carry ourselves.

How do we get it?

Know yourself.

Know and respect others.

Self-awareness helps us build self-confidence, self-respect, and our self-worth. These things in turn help us learn to respect others.

If character is any one thing, I think it is about how we treat other people. It is about respecting all of humanity and respecting the individual, including his/her foibles. When someone says of another person, "They have character," I think they are saying, "She understands, respects, and appreciates others."

If you want to 'have character' think about this.

# 47. Identity

Synonyms: uniqueness; distinctive; individuality; distinguished

Antonyms: not distinctive; not unique; run of the mill; undistinguished; unmemorable

We are all unique. We all have our own identity. This word isn't important because it is something we lack, but because it is something worth thinking about.

How are we unique, distinctive?

I love the word uniqueness. I almost chose it instead of identity, but identity is perhaps a bit broader. Our whole identity includes our uniqueness as well as our 'sameness.'

> In writing this book I had to think about why this work would be different from the many other similar types of books on the market. I had to think about how what I brought to the table was unique.
>
> I believe it is my ability to think and write from a more educational perspective. While I did a great deal of background research, that is not necessarily unique. And while I write in a practical, down-to-earth style, which hopefully is refreshing and somewhat rare, it is not completely unique. But I believe there are few other business writers with my extensive educational and educational-writing background. That is what helps create my unique identity as an author, coach, presenter, and business writer and speaker.

Thinking about and delineating what makes us unique and distinctive as a manager/leader is very important. It is well worth putting some time and effort into. In the process we understand more about ourselves and how others see us.

Identity is about perspective. It can be our own perspective of who we are, but just as importantly it is understanding how others see us.

When I told one of the members of my team that I was going to revise all the materials available online at www.difficultpeople.org and firm them up a bit, he said, "Don't change the way you write things, that is what makes this stuff good." Another team member refers to the best elements of my style as 'Koobish.'

Understanding and staying alert to how others see us, gives us the advantage of being able to work on our character and identity when we see things we (they) don't like, and to build on the things we (they) do like.

"Image is everything."

(Quote from a commercial with Andre Agassi, tennis player)

Image may not be everything, but perspective certainly plays a huge role in life. How others see us may be, and often is, very different from how we see ourselves. I have learned a lot about myself by having the courage to see myself from others' eyes and to be willing to take the plunge and ask, when I couldn't quite understand how I was coming across. Knowing yourself from another's perspective can be very eye-opening.

Knowing yourself from an 'enemy's' point of view can tell us a great deal, too. We may not feel they are right, but whatever they feel and think IS who we are to them. It is their version of the real 'you.' When we are aware of how they feel and think, we can make positive choices that make a difference in how they see us and in how we interact with them. It can be achieved by working with their concerns, by understanding what is important to them, and by reaching a better understanding of each other. When we are able to appreciate their uniqueness and their identity we have changed in their eyes.

Identity involves learning: learning about ourselves through self-observation; learning about others; and learning about how others perceive us. Then it is about how we work to improve who we are through this knowledge.

Be unique: not because you need to be different from others, but because you are. Relish your uniqueness and allow it to be your gift to the rest of the world.

# PART VI
# Quality

"Quality begins precisely with emotional attachment,

no ifs, ands, or buts."

(Peters, *Thriving On Chaos*)

# 48. Quality

Synonyms: excellence; class; superior; value

Antonyms: inferior; poor; lesser; mediocre

If you talked with a great many managers, leaders, and executives, you would come to believe that everyone considers quality to be of the utmost importance. However, with quality, the proof is in the results. I could list a half dozen companies that I have dealt with in the past WEEK that I feel have failed on quality. Some companies, based on the responses one gets from their customer service personnel, don't seem to care, or may give lip service to quality but don't really do anything about it. These are big name companies who <u>should</u> be concerned with quality and customer service: major retailers, large banks, delivery services, etc.

Quality is present only when and if you and other people

recognize it, and recognize it, and recognize it....

"Starting this afternoon, don't walk past a shoddy product or service without comment and action – ever again!"[Peters, *Thriving on Chaos* (There are some excellent sections in this book on Quality)]

Quality comes from leaders who are committed to it. They exhibit it in their own work, they expect it from others, and they make sure it is happening. Unfortunately, a personal commitment to quality is not enough in the short run. With the high turnover of managers (and their subordinates) in industry today the short run may be all you have.

Yes, a leader committed to quality may make an impact and over time will certainly influence the quality of the products and/or services coming from his group. However, if she is there trying to make changes to a group ingrained in mediocre performance, there will be a great deal of resistance, grumbling, and wasted time in that long process of change.

Great leaders must walk and talk quality at every opportunity. Make it a priority in everything you do and in everything you talk about. Quality will become everyone's issue when they see it is your issue. It will happen faster only when you tell them, show them, and retell them. (Also, see Chapter 40 on Visibility)

Quality is everyone's, and I mean everyone's, responsibility. If your custodians aren't keeping the place clean, that reflects on overall quality. It reflects on pride and pride is essential to good quality. If one of your telemarketers gets away with a perfunctory attitude, someone will know, and they will tell others, and then others. A manager who lets things slide will find his whole team beginning to let things slide.

Quality is caring what comes out of your group. If people don't care, then the product suffers. It is getting people involved in being and doing their best – not just for you, not just for the company, but also for themselves. Pride in something well done is a good thing. It doesn't elevate someone above another but creates an aura of 'can do,' and can-do-again.

> I remember reading Ayn's Rand's works many years ago (*The Fountainhead, Atlas Shrugged*, etc.) and she talked about quality a good bit. There was always a sense of 'if you are going to do something, however mundane, do it the best you possibly can.'

As managers we too often focus on judging and evaluation. Quality comes more from, "How can we make or do this better?" "How can we be the 'best we can be.'" And perhaps most importantly, "How can I contribute my best to making things better."

Quality is something we must live and breathe if we are truly on board. Getting a team on board quality is a thing of beauty in and of itself. When people care, things happen. Great managers help their team members add **value** (see next chapter).

Great leaders help their personnel to stretch themselves (see Chapter 50).

**Truly great leaders care.**

# 49. Value-added

Synonyms: value; worth; merit; best

Antonyms: poor; reduced; cheap

Value-added has become a bit of an over-used byword in the business world today, but it is still a useful term. Value-added means, in the best possible interpretation, "a thousand things done a little bit better." (Peters and Austin, *A Passion for Excellence*).

When we think of adding value piece by piece, task by task, moment by moment, it becomes something that everyone can easily be a part of. "Making this the best automobile ever," may be a great ideal and goal, but to everyone in the trenches, including all the line and matrix managers, it is so 'up there' as to have little more than a pie-in-the-sky meaning.

In some ways the same logic can be applied to visions and strategies. Visions that motivate a team are important, as are strategies that help us reach and believe in our vision. But the true work comes from the tightening of the nuts and bolts that we do on a moment to moment basis. If one nut on an automobile is not tightened properly it may affect the whole performance and safety of that vehicle. Yet it is just one nut of thousands, isn't it?

Everyone's responsibility is that one nut. Value-added means making sure all nuts are tightened to specs. Or it could be designing a better nut so specific tightening parameters may not be an issue. It might be finding something that works better than a nut for that particular situation. And so on.

Value-added is making everyone a contributor to the quality of a product or service. There are almost always improved ways we can do things. One customer service representative may find the best way to handle a specific complaint and share it with his teammates. Another may discover an easier way to pass on information or to revise a weighty form or to eliminate a layer in the process of resolving issues. Be open to the possibilities that everyone on your team has to offer.

Value-added is about responsibility, creativity and innovation, i.e. improving quality. It is about encouraging, not just allowing, people to think for themselves.

THIS is a moment that you and your team can add value to your product. Make the most of it!

# 50. Stretching

Synonyms: extending; making bigger and better; drawing out

Antonyms: shrinking; lessening; attenuation; dwindling

This is a great word – it has an immediate visual component and an auditory one as well. Just saying the word, s-t-r-e-t-c-h, brings to mind the value of this term.

Stretching from a leadership perspective is just how the word feels and sounds – going beyond one's normal parameters. The key to stretching for a leader is opening up the space for his team to stretch in.

As a coach I often see a great deal of reluctance on the part of managers to let their employees have more leeway in which to operate. Great teams are built on trust and responsibility and they should have a certain amount of give and take as a result. Team members won't show what they can accomplish unless we give them room. When they take that room and run with it, we can give them even more room. If they fail, then we use that opportunity to help them learn from their mistakes and give them other opportunities, perhaps different, perhaps the same, in which to succeed.

Creating more space for a team member doesn't take away space or responsibility from you as a leader. If anything, it expands your own sphere because more is happening and more is getting accomplished. Managers who allow their team members room to grow and blossom are often the ones who shine themselves.

Potentially great team players will quickly pick up on opportunities they have to improve and expand their horizons. Other players on the same team will likely be influenced by how they see their compatriots performing and succeeding.

Stretching comes in many forms: learning, education, and training (see next Chapter and 52), creativity and innovation (see 73 and 74), experimentation and risk-taking (76 and 77) and generally more flexibility to find better ways of doing things (see 75). It can also simply be a feeling that pervades a group that adds to their motivation and momentum because it is just 'there' – ready to be taken advantage of if the opportunity or idea presents itself.

Stretching is the opposite of complacency. The astute manager will, as Peters points out, '...eschew complacency like the plague." (*Professional Service Firm 50*)

Great leaders also know how important it is to s-t-r-e-t-c-h themselves. Challenge yourself to find ways to stretch every day. Sometimes it is just those little extra efforts we make that make all the difference.

# 51. Learning

Synonyms: education; knowledge

Antonyms: status quo

I am passionate about learning. For as long as I can remember it has been a focal point of my life. My brothers and I used to play school when we were young kids, I taught my first music lesson at ten, and I have been in education in one way or another ever since then. Learning is as fundamental to me as breathing.

The most important thing I think I have learned about learning is this: every circumstance and interaction I find myself in has the opportunity for me to learn something.

Leaders have the opportunity to build a foundation about the importance of learning into their work vision and strategy. An important question a leader needs to learn to ask on a regular basis is, "How can we learn from this?" And he/she needs to apply that question to both the bad and the good, the mistakes and failures, as well as the successes.

John Dewey, the great American educator, believed in learning through experience. Book learnin' is a wonderful way to dispense information and knowledge, but we learn best by doing.

In his book *Experience and Education*, Dewey states,

> "The belief that all genuine education comes about through
>
> Experience does not mean that all experiences
>
> are genuinely or equally educative..."

Leaders prepare the ground for education and learning by their attitude and by the way they handle difficulties, mistakes, and change.

When we approach our work life with a deep regard for learning from every avenue possible, we instill an attitude that is proactive instead of reactive. If I put down or 'evaluate' an employee because of their failures, I have taught very little except fear or avoidance. When I turn those opportunities into learning experiences I can potentially build a valuable team member and a dedicated employee.

There are as many ways to learn as there are people on our team – more, in fact. Learning isn't so much fitting people into a mold so they produce more of something or create something better, as it is opening up the possibilities, so they take advantage of what can be learned.

Leaders not only encourage learning, they exemplify it. They take what is thrown at them, and not only deal with it, but learn from it. We can study with the best teachers in the world, but the fundamental truth is that

'One's best teacher is himself (herself).'

[I don't know if I said this originally, or whether I read it somewhere many, many years ago, but it was on my bulletin board for students to see for the twenty-something years that I taught college.]

Learning from experiences at work, both positive and negative, can be great motivators. It can help turn problem employees into contributing group members. It can light a fire under talented employees who have just been treading water. It does take some foresight and staying on top of opportunities. An important question to ask is, "What have we learned from this?" Looking back at what has been accomplished also helps, and it sets the stage for further learning.

# 52. Education

Synonyms: instruction; guidance; preparation

Antonyms: stagnate; decline; stand still

"Education is...a fostering, a nurturing, a cultivating process."

(Dewey, *Democracy and Education*)

Education, or as we refer to it in the business world, 'training,' is an important part of maintaining and improving a team's outlook and performance. Unfortunately education is too often canned experiences forced upon teams or groups by managers or Human Resources departments who feel personnel need this so that the business is 'covering its butt,' or because it 'seemed like a good thing at the time.'

From my standpoint as an educator, the best of education and training comes from the team or group leader. She knows what is best for her personnel and can work to provide it. She also can generate input from team members on what issues they feel they could use training in. If time management is a major issue within her department or managerial staff, then she would be wise to find an educational experience led by someone who has a good feel for her business and who is willing to make the effort to tailor the training to her group's needs.

You may be able to tell that I am not a huge supporter of 'tried and true' methodologies. I am not, unless they are in the hands of an educator who is willing to make the effort to work the materials into a format that is best for the group he or she will be teaching/training. Canned presentations leave out the human factor and don't have the flexibility to adjust to the circumstances or the people involved. I AM all in favor of training people in ideas and knowledge and then letting them apply it in the best way possible for their business, approach, and style.

One size really doesn't fit all!

Education, from my perspective, has to have flexibility and freedom as a fundamental part of the curriculum. Otherwise it doesn't fit John Dewey's definition above of "a fostering, nurturing, and cultivating process."

Taking time management as an issue and as an example:

> We understand the need to manage our time.
>
> We pretty much believe we do the best we can under the circumstances.
>
> We are resistant to changing anything, even when we know we should.

Good time management courses and its instructors know these caveats from the outset and they build their programs around the potential resistances they will meet. Plus they incorporate specific information and ideas related to the team and business they will be working with into their solutions for that team. If they are wise, they build in many choices that allow the team players to have some control of how they improve their own situation.

Training is also a means of renewal. High stress jobs tend to have a high turnover rate because employees lose sight of the fundamentals and motivation they had going in.

**As an example**

Customer service representatives can benefit from brief, refresher seminars that are motivationally-based. Educational reminders of this sort can be a tremendous resource for quality employees who just need a brief change of pace to get them back into the swing of things. Education is often not something new so much as it is saying 'old stuff' in new ways, so that we remind ourselves of what is important in our work and life.

I used to tell my students, "I can teach you everything you need to know (in this particular discipline) in one semester. The next seven semesters and the rest of your life will be spent in learning how to actually apply that knowledge." Education often is simply a cultivation of knowledge we already have to make it more and more useful and more applicable to our current needs.

Education should also include choices. Employees who are self-motivated will often take opportunities to expand themselves if they are made available to them. Great benefit can result if organizational and business leaders make educational opportunities available.

> One of the largest organizations in the world, the U.S. military, saw the importance of this many, many years ago. My dad got both his Bachelor's degree and his Master's degree through the military as well as a lot of other training and education. The military has long recognized the importance of providing education for all its personnel and extended educational opportunities for its motivated and talented employees.

Self-motivated education and training should also be encouraged and supported. If I were leading a business team, I would find a way to budget materials, time, and book tuition for employees who were interested in expanding their education in pretty much any direction. Whether they are studying basket-weaving or marketing, education helps motivate and keep people young and vibrant. I might be more willing to support certain types of programs over others, but keeping employees happy and motivated is no small thing at any point and often the rewards associated with these small outlays of funds are far greater than what it costs.

When we are not learning, we are pretty much standing still or even declining.

Choose to move ahead and choose to support that with your team.

Choose education, you will be glad you did.

# 53. Renewal

Synonyms: regeneration; restoration; revitalization; rebirth

Antonyms: stagnate; rot; decline

Renewal is a big step past education, or even reeducation. Renewal has to do with how we feel about ourselves and our job. We certainly can use training, education, seminars, and formal presentations as a means of renewal for employees, but there is so much more that we can do.

In many ways the entire second section of this book, which focuses on "Service to Others," is about renewal. We can help employees renew their energy, commitment, and performance through acknowledgment, appreciation, support, recognition, and rewards.

We can do it best by paying attention to the small things:

Finding out about and eliminating those small irritants that are in every workplace

Saying thanks, just because

Remembering birthdays and holidays

Being kind, especially when we take the time to notice when someone is down

Smiling and eliciting a smile

Complimenting

Showing interest

Giving a small gift

Taking a break – and encouraging others to take a break

Having a meeting outdoors instead of in that stuffy office

A memo that says I am glad you are here

Sharing your donut

Sharing yourself – something about who you are as a person; take a chance (Even if you are the boss!)

There are a thousand little things that can say, "I care," or "Let me help," or "What can I do to make your day, week, month, better?" Just asking can change the whole dynamics of a person's day.

We all get bogged down in the every-day-ness of every day. It is all too easy to slip into worry, frustration, depressive moods, and so on. Every once in a while I meet someone who literally lights up a room. While it would be great if we could all have that type of personality, we can still make a difference with the people we interact with by focusing on the positive. It only takes a small effort. It takes:

Acknowledging and appreciating people

Saying 'thank you' often

Sincere compliments

Recognizing people and their efforts

Kind words and kind gestures

Compassion

Caring

What it does take is my reminding myself that others appreciate these small gestures and when I make this effort it is a form of tremendous renewal for myself as well. Every effort I make for another comes back to me many-fold.

Renewal is for yourself and for others. Take care of you. Take care of them. You will have far fewer concerns and problems as a result. You will be surprised at the quality of work that results, too!

# 54. Solution-focused

Synonyms: responsible; result; outcome

Antonyms: blaming; complaining; whining; not responsible

Solution-focused is another byword of industry that has become a bit jaded with overuse. The truth is that this is a great way to approach work. It is also a terrific way to deal with concerns, problems, change, and difficult people.

Significant change within or to a team or organization can and often does create a tremendous amount of angst. People may feel lost, out-of-control, threatened, in shock, and they will very likely experience other physical and mental reactions as well, such as becoming more prone to illness, depression, anxiety, and so on. Solutions are rarely easy; nor do they happen quickly. But the wise manager leads his personnel toward action, toward solutions.

Sometimes solution-focused action is and should be very short-term. It is important to get people moving in a positive direction with short term goals and quick success. Then keep them as informed as possible throughout the change process or difficulty and lead them through the next phase, toward the next goal. Work to get them involved in the process of developing the next action/solution phase. This gives your team a foundation of control upon which positive solutions for the long term can be built.

The same techniques can be applied very successfully with difficult people and/or difficult situations. Blaming, complaining, and otherwise negative personnel undermine the whole atmosphere of a group, and they can do it very quickly. Lead them out of their negative self-focus and insecurity by insisting on their being catalysts for their own change and development. Involve them with finding solutions to their concerns rather than allowing them to wallow in their misery and spreading their misery to others.

Often this process has to start with small incremental performance improvements and quickly achievable goals. Initially pay close attention to their successes and failures. Give them frequent supervision and support. Remember to reward successes and to treat concerns as learning experiences with renewed focus and effort as part of the new solution. As they improve their performance and approach, give them more and more independence and responsibility and be sure to let them know that their new approach to work is the reason for their success and reward.

Successful leaders deal with difficulties and negativity up front and right away. Make sure that team members understand that nothing short of a solution-focused mentality in dealing with all types of issues is critical to good leadership. Not dealing with these types of concerns or putting them on the back burner can create much more serious developmental and attitudinal concerns down the road.

Solution-focus is quality-centered. Quality is the value and a solution-focused approach is one of the means of achieving that value.

# 55. Catalyst

Synonyms: mechanism; accelerator; vehicle; facilitator

Antonyms: naysayer; cynic; pessimist

Characteristics of a Catalyst: intuitive; communicative; passionate; talented; creative; initiating; responsible; generous; influential (from *The 17 Indisputable Laws of Teamwork*, Maxwell)

A catalyst helps get things done. If you have a stick of dynamite in your hand you have the potential to make a really big bang, but nothing much will happen unless you have a blasting cap or fuse to set it off. Leaders, great leaders, perhaps more than any other role they perform, are catalysts for moving their teams forward and in the right direction.

Whether one is the manager of a department of two or the vice president of a 400 person group, the concept is the same.

I particularly enjoyed reading Lou Gerstner's book, *Who Said Elephants Can't Dance?* Lou took over as Chairman and CEO of IBM when it was having major adjustment problems in the 1980s and 1990s. Throughout the book a number of clear concepts emerged that showed his mettle as a leader. One of those, though he didn't specifically delineate it himself, is that he made things happen. He was the catalyst that IBM needed to change from a stodgy old bureaucracy to a streamlined organization capable of competing in the challenging and constantly changing business environment today.

How did he do it?

Self-confidence, determination, quality-focused, persistence, and awareness to name a few traits that come to mind. He believed in what he was trying to do, he got the right people on the bus and the wrong people off the bus (Collins), he believed in the people and company that IBM was, and he believed, ultimately and fundamentally in himself. He was able to be a catalyst because he believed in himself and what he was doing.

One other key idea: he had the guts to go for it once he made up his mind to take the job. There was no second guessing (see Chapter 90 on **Courage**).

Leaders who are catalysts know what they are about and they believe in getting things done. They move ahead and they get others moving. As a coach I have seen too many potentially great leaders fail as catalysts for change and progress because they lacked the courage to push through for what they believed in.

Catalysts know there is a risk. They know that every time they push forward an idea or strategy that there is a chance it may fail, and without the inner conviction and courage that they bring to the process it would more than likely fail. Catalysts take chances; they make things happen. (See Chapters 77, **Risk-taking**, and 70, **Chances**).

> There ain't gonna be any boom
>
> unless you are there to set the fuse.

The other very interesting thing about being a catalyst is that it is fun. (Maxwell and Koob)

# 56. Cultivate

Synonyms: nurture; grow; promote

Antonyms: demoralize; discourage; reject; put off; disavow; disallow; discard

When I read Voltaire's *Candide,* I was immediately struck by the famous line, "We must cultivate our gardens." Cultivate is such a descriptive word. To cultivate takes finesse. It is not just plowing or harrowing or seeding, it is all of those and something more. It implies, for me, 'taking care of,' or perhaps even better, 'taking care with.'

### "Cultivate your people"

This might have been something my dad would have said if he had ever read Voltaire, because that is one of the things as a manager that he was remarkable at. He took care of and took care with the people who worked for him and with him. It is perhaps an unusual trait for a career military man and later the vice president of a bank, but if you want to know what he meant to 'his people' go to Hopkinsville, KY and ask just about anyone about Colonel Koob. That is what cultivating means to me in the sense of leadership.

Leaders cultivate. They don't just grow, or train, or mentor – they take care of, and care with, the people they are responsible for.

Mentoring, and especially the relatively new coaching profession, are closest to the concept of cultivating. A good coach focuses on building and working with a client's strengths, helps them as they work through concerns and weaknesses, and offers a great deal of encouragement and support. Ideally a good mentor does the same thing. However, in my experience as a coach and through my association with current business practices, the reality is far from this paragon.

# Dr. Joseph Koob

Typically a new employee may be assigned a mentor who meets with their 'mentee' once or twice, gives them the rundown and then the association pretty much ends. Occasionally the mentor will check up on their comrade-in-arms, but at most it is a casual lunch, and often it is simply a "How are you doing?" as they pass in the hallway or maybe a quick phone call.

Leaders can be good coaches. A wise leader will dig out a few books on the subject and get a handle at least on the way coaches approach clients and some of the ideas, skills, and techniques they use. A really wise leader will have a coach, at least for a time, to get thoroughly familiar with how the profession works and the benefits it can produce.

> Just as an example: I have never coached a manager or executive who didn't feel they gained a tremendous amount from the process (and I don't know of anyone who coached with someone else, either, who didn't realize great benefits).

Coaches cultivate. I think it is a good, if not, the best descriptor for the profession. It is far different than counseling and it is a valuable tool for leaders to use. They can learn some of the skills themselves – a very good idea; and they can hire coaches to work with their personnel.

However, there is also the general day to day aspect of cultivating, that my dad had, that doesn't come from a book or from skills learned from a coach. It comes from the heart.

**If you don't care about people,**

**you shouldn't be a leader.**

# 57. Rigorous

Synonyms: thorough; precise; accurate; meticulous; painstaking; careful

Antonyms: inexact; undemanding; unchallenging; vague; imprecise; approximate

There is nothing wishy-washy about a good leader. Underneath that kind, caring, humble service-to-others persona is a person who cares about quality, who cares about getting things done and getting them done right, and who doesn't brook any nonsense or give anything less than 110% effort.

Rigorous is another good descriptive word. It says more in one word than any other single word I could come up with. Good leaders are rigorous, first and foremost, in their own work. Their employees and team members may not see it at first. They don't necessarily directly observe their boss coming in early and leaving late, taking work home and spending hours accomplishing things into the wee hours, or coming in regularly on weekends, but if they pay attention, and they will, they will see it in everything they do and in every way that they demand quality from others.

A manager cannot demand the utmost from her employees unless she exemplifies it in her own work ethic. Rigorousness is excellence and effort in her own work, as well as in what she expects from others."

As a coach I have seen 'rigorous' leaders take over less than energetic teams and watched from the sidelines as the team transformed itself. It doesn't happen immediately and there is often some resistance at first, but gradually the whole atmosphere of the team changes – a new dynamism and care for quality emerges.

The managers didn't have to directly teach them to be more rigorous. They didn't jump all over them when they didn't quite measure up. More than anything else they exhibited what they expected. They corrected and cajoled along the way, and they demanded the best from themselves and from the team when they had to deliver.

In many ways rigorousness is about being able to deliver the best that everyone has to offer. It is paying attention to quality. It is not putting up with complacency, the mediocre, or the mundane.

When rigorousness permeates a team, it changes the dynamics of the members' interactions, it energizes everyone's efforts, it provides focus and goal-directedness, and it instigates pride and motivation. It is a powerful force that comes from the quality-centered behavior of a unique personality.

**Being rigorous means quality in everything you do.**

# PART VII
# Personal Approach

Qualities that leaders possess and exemplify in their work.

# 58. Persistence

Synonyms: determination; doggedness; perseverance

Antonyms: give up; undetermined; irresolute; uncertain; wavering

I like the terms 'doggedness,' and tenacity,' but persistence is a bit more familiar and doesn't quite have the 'stubbornness' implied by these other two. 'Singlemindedness' is also a good term that has overtones of focus, but is a bit too narrow for this purpose. Persistence says 'stick-to-it-tive-ness' and if that were an easily acceptable word I would use that instead.

I think there is a quality about great leaders that does remind me of a dog grabbing on to something with his jaws, unwilling to let go. Winston Churchill had this quality. Ulysses S. Grant had it. And from everything I have read, General Patton exemplified this.

Leaders show determination and stick-to-it-tive-ness. They don't back off at the first signs of trouble, and they especially don't quit or give in when they run into a roadblock to something they sincerely believe in. [Important: I have seen otherwise excellent leaders who seem to have some trouble in this area.]

Persistence is very much tied up with pushing for, working with, finding ways to get done what needs to be done, and most importantly, doing what one believes should be done.

Persistence is guided effort. It is not bulldogging through your own agenda in spite of everyone else. It is not about ignoring suggestions and canning others' ideas. Persistence takes intelligence and consideration.

Persistence is also about quality. If it isn't wrapped up in quality, it is probably mis-guided effort. Maybe more than just quality, persistence is about a belief in quality. We persist with an idea and with effort because we believe in it. It has meaning for us, and for our vision, and our team.

I think this is one thing that drives an individual's persistence – a vision of what he is striving for. Visions can be global (see Chapter 88) or they can be more focused, a part of the larger vision, but more immediately achievable. When I conceive of a goal and can envision, create an image in my mind, of the outcome, it provides direction for my effort. Persistence grows from an ability to develop a clear idea of what one wishes to achieve.

Persistence can become a part of a team's effort when a leader can provide that clarity of purpose for his team.

# 59. Synthesizer

Synonyms: combine; cohesive; bring together; glue

Antonyms: break down; take apart; unglue

One of my professors in graduate school often emphasized the concept of **'synthesis, analysis, synthesis'** in approaching education.

[Dr. Charles Leonhard, University of Illinois at Urbana-Champaign, *Foundations and Principles of Music Education*)]

The basic idea is that we need first to provide a global picture of what we want to teach – as in the adage about being unable to see the forest because of the trees (i.e. take a look at the forest). Then we analyze the elements that will help us understand the concept of 'forest' better (perhaps by studying different types of trees and plants). Then we step back once more and look at the whole again in a new light. (We understand 'forest' better as a result.)

There is much that we do in industry that has to do with the pieces of things (analysis), and often not much that has to do with the whole (synthesis). A manager has the opportunity to bring things together. This can be about vision, strategy, and motivation. It can also be about giving players a perspective of why and how their efforts make a difference. I think this is one way a leader can add value – by synthesizing things and ideas that make a difference to his team, especially those things that make a difference in how they feel about their jobs and what they are accomplishing.

Unfortunately too often we assume that people 'get it,' i.e. that there is no need to bring things together. People, however, like to be appreciated and acknowledged. Synthesis of ideas and effort is a form of acknowledgment. By showing outcomes and the forward movement of pieces of the puzzle, one is recognizing how these small accomplishments fit into the whole and add to the ultimate vision and goals of not only the team but the business.

A good leader can not only keep members focused on the important work they do, but can give them feedback and encouragement based on the overall vision and goals they are actually working for. People can share in the progress and success of a product if they understand how what they do fits into the big picture and if they are vested in the outcome by the quality of the finished product.

Synthesis of ideas and effort can take place at many levels. Whatever level of an organization a manager works on, there are ways to bring things together that can help focus and motivate team members. Information serves many purposes. When it can help motivate and direct personnel, it is worth sharing.


Be a synthesizer for your players. They will probably appreciate it,

**they will learn something,**

**and you will too.**

# 60. Cohesion

Synonyms: glue; stickiness; sticking together; union

Antonyms: separate; apart; loose; disunion, dissolution

Coherence:

> "Each piece of the system reinforces the other parts of the system
> to form an integrated whole that is much more powerful
> than the sum of the parts."
>
> (Collins, *Good to Great*)

When I think of cohesion, I think of a team. One of the things leaders should keep in mind is the importance of developing cohesiveness within their groups. This is particularly essential for mid-level managers who are working directly with reasonable-sized teams (up to 50). But it should also be kept in mind regardless of the size of the group or organization for which you are responsible.

Cohesiveness, working together, camaraderie, develops as a natural outcome of people working close together toward a common goal. The more focused and intense the work, the more likely teamwork and relationship will develop. Cohesion is also related to the leader's style and approach to leadership. Many of the terms we have discussed so far have a marked impact on how a team gathers together around a common goal and leadership.

Another very critical concept that will be discussed later is 'Passion.' (See Chapter 87) When a leader has tremendous focus and desire, it does affect the cohesion, momentum, and dynamics of the team he leads.

Involvement is part of how people see themselves in relationship to the group, in relationship to the goals and vision of the team, and in relationship to the team's leader. A team member who does not see themselves as an integral part of the effort the team is making, will not become a cohesive player, working with others toward a common goal, the common good.

Leaders need to be vigilant for negativity that can destroy a team's unity. There is a certain amount of natural rivalry and competitiveness that is good for everyone and often good for driving performance. However, negativity, disgruntledness, constant complaining and blaming can quickly divide a productive team into warring factions.

It is good to encourage healthy rivalries, experimentation and innovation, risk-taking, and even irreverent fun. These are ways that teams build cohesiveness.

People generally work together because they have to. They work well together by choice. It is never a given. I have yet to see a team of more than three members who didn't have occasional conflicts, disagreements, and significant personality differences. However, even with these very typical conditions that can (and sometimes do) become serious concerns, many groups, especially those led by strong, quality-focused leadership become cohesive, dynamic forces in spite of themselves and their differences.

It takes a leader who cares and who pays attention when attention is warranted.

# 61. Attitude

Synonyms: approach; outlook; stance; position; mind-set; image
Antonyms: poor image

How do you feel right now?

If you think about your work right this minute, how do you feel about it?

How do you feel about getting up and going to work every morning?

How do you feel about going to work on a Monday morning?

How do you feel when you are at work – every day?

Believe it or not, the way you answer these questions is the attitude you are more than likely showing to your colleagues and employees. It is worth spending some time thinking seriously about this.

> "Attitude is catching....People always project on the outside
>
> how they feel on the inside.
>
> Attitude is really about how a person is."
>
> (Maxwell, *The 17 Indisputable Laws of Teamwork*)

We all know what attitude is. We recognize a bad attitude almost immediately. We can easily point our fingers at various people we know and say, "That is a rotten way to look at the world." What we don't see, unless we really pay attention, is our own attitude and how it affects others.

It takes a good bit of courage to admit that we need an attitude adjustment. It takes a great deal of courage to ask others how we come across.

I have a saying that I initially wrote in my book, *A Perfect Day: Guide for a Better Life* that says a great deal about attitude.

"If you are not having fun, something's wrong."

Sometimes I add the postscript, "Adjust."

**"If you are not having fun, something's wrong – adjust!"**

If we are seriously not enjoying our work and our life, something IS wrong and we do need to make adjustments. If we don't, we will be dragging others down with us. It is virtually guaranteed.

Attitude is not something that comes from without. It is a choice we make. A choice that is wrapped up in many choices we have made throughout our lives. It is a habit, and will remain just that, unless we start paying attention to who we are and how we come across to the world. Attitude is about taking ownership of our lives (see Chapter 4). If we blame circumstances and problems on others, it is a choice we make. We can make another choice, and that is to take responsibility for who we are and how we impact the world, regardless of what comes from the outside to impact us.

I have never met a person who didn't have problems and concerns. I don't think there are many people on this earth who haven't had bad things happen, who haven't had to struggle with major issues and through very difficult times. What I do know is that there are people who face their issues and conflicts with all the courage and strength they can muster and there are others who would much rather place the blame on others, the world, God, or anything else, as long as it isn't their responsibility.

Your attitude is your responsibility. If you can't accept that, then please don't try to lead others. You will fail. Leaders lead by example. Positivity is so much better than negativity.

"The winner's edge is all about attitude, not aptitude."

(Maxwell, *The 21 Indispensible Laws of Leadership)*


Try these questions on for size:


How do your players feel right now?

If you think about them at work right this minute, how do you think they feel about it?

How do they feel about getting up and going to work every morning?

How do they feel about going to work on a Monday morning?

How do they feel when they are at work – every day?


**"If they are not having fun, something's wrong –**

**Can you help them adjust?"**

# 62. Consistent

Synonyms: reliable; steady; dependable; constant

Antonyms: inconsistent; contradictory; unreliable; unpredictable

No one likes inconsistency. We abhor managers who change their tune because of the way the tide is flowing, who can't make up their minds, or who vacillate from one day to another in how they treat people.

While I almost hate to bring this up, generally we actually prefer someone who is more negative, but consistent, than someone who is a bright pleasant personality one minute and a tyrant the next. We would rather know what is coming than have to be on our toes all the time waiting for the next explosion.

> We don't like unreliable people.
>
> We are frustrated to distraction by contradiction.
>
> We wish everything could be predictable...well almost everything.
>
> We like having a safe harbor in a storm.

Consistency is concerned on many levels with control. A leader who is consistent in his approach to problems, personnel concerns, evaluation processes, planning and strategy, and so on, sets up a 'system' in essence that everyone can become familiar with. That type of control is a rock upon which everyone can stand when change, disruption, and difficult issues impact a team's stability.

Another good word that reflects this is 'constancy.' We like things in life that are constant. Human beings are, even the most freedom-loving and creative of us, organizing creatures. We like to place things into neat little piles so that when we work with them or use them, they are just where and how we left them. A leader who is constant in many ways helps all of the members of his team feel rooted in some type of structure that is comfortable and stable in spite of all the turmoil that may surround them...as Chevy says, "Like a Rock."

Later in this book we will discuss creativity, innovation, flexibility, experimentation, risk-taking and other related topics. (see Part VIII, "FREE Yourself!") As a creative-type myself, I am all for throwing caution to the wind and jumping into new things with both feet and arms spread wide. However, there is a great deal of merit to providing structure and consistency as a foundation for taking chances and for creating freely.

Leaders exemplify many things:

> A constancy of purpose

> A consistent approach to dealing with problems and concerns

> A solid belief in who they are and what they are about

These attributes help them to create an environment in which employees can be safe, secure, and comfortable.

Never lose sight of the fact that when push comes to shove, your team looks up to you for help, support, and constancy. As much as they like their independence,

**you are who they turn to when things get difficult.**

# 63. Cooperative

Synonyms: accommodating; helpful; supportive

Antonyms: unhelpful; uncooperative; obstructive; disruptive

While leaders certainly need to cooperate with many people throughout their working and industry framework, I selected this word more from the standpoint of having the skill and talent to get others to be cooperative, especially under trying circumstances.

It would be nice, very nice, if everyone got along on a team and there were no personality bumps in the road. Unfortunately that is rarely the case. Even in relatively small teams (3 to 10 players) there is often some, and sometimes a lot, of disagreement and dissension. Discord because of ill feelings can cause major disruptions at work, including backbiting, backstabbing, and negative turf wars.

Disagreement can be healthy if it comes from an effort to achieve the best possible solutions to concerns and problems. People don't always have to get along or even like each other, but it is important that they respect each others boundaries and contributions.

Leadership is about leading. Most of this book is about the qualities leaders can develop to help them lead by example and by their overall approach and style. Many people will get on board with you because of who you are and how you do things. However, there are always a few whose self-worth is so poor that their insecurity creates tremendous angst and many concerns. Good leaders learn the skills needed to deal with these types of problems.

This book does not have the scope to teach you how to deal with uncooperative, difficult employees. However, immediately below I will outline some of the key ideas that leaders can use to deal with these types of concerns.

Above all else, pay attention. The more you understand the dynamics that have caused friction to develop, the easier it will be to seek solutions. Keep in mind that uncooperative employees are motivated by many things. They see themselves in an entirely different light than the people they work with and very likely from the way you see them.

Many difficult people don't understand how they are coming across to others. They don't see themselves as being difficult. (Koob, *Understanding and Working with Difficult People*) Making the effort to understand who they are and where they are coming from is very important. The extra attention is often all they really want.

Bring everything to the table. Openness about feelings and thoughts may be painful to bring out in the open, but keeping things hidden only lets them fester more. Get the people involved talking, one-on-one, together, with a coach, etc.

Be solution-oriented and get everyone else involved on board. When people are encouraged to seek solutions and nothing less than a solution-oriented approach is acceptable, they will more than likely make the effort to get back on the bus, or they will get off the bus entirely (and seek another job.)

Structure is key. Often, if we step back from quarrels and concerns between people, we see that there is a childish aspect to their interactions. Setting up guidelines and parameters for difficult employees, if necessary through the evaluation process, gives you and them something concrete to work from. It also gives you and them a way to measure progress.

Be positive in the face of whatever negativity is being tossed around. Your self-worth, self-confidence, and self-control can add tremendously to the overall picture. Negativity doesn't stand much of a chance in the face of real positivity. This can be very difficult to maintain, especially with arguing, infighting employees, but it does make a big difference in your ability to handle the situation.

Be firm and in control when you need to be. A no-nonsense position when it comes to integrity, honesty, and responsibility is a must.

Embedded rivalries and difficult people don't 'get better' over night. Follow-up is very important. Improvements should be rewarded and slip-ups need to be monitored and reevaluated with improved strategies and solution-oriented programs.

Poor personal dynamics are systemic. It is never just one person. One very negative employee may have been the initial catalyst and may still be the major player in the concerns brought out by the team, but everyone plays a role and needs to be onboard the solution. Ask almost any difficult person who is being difficult and they will point to someone (or everyone) else on the team.

Cultivate an employee's strengths and help them work on their weaknesses. Major difficulties are sometimes solved fairly readily by reorienting a 'problem' child to an area where they can succeed, and where they can receive more positive attention. Often difficult people are seeking attention, appreciation, acknowledgment, and recognition. We can't give it to them for being 'bad,' but we can seek ways to give them legitimate opportunities to succeed.

Be there. Visibility works wonders. When people see that you care and are concerned about the dynamics of the group, they will likely seek solutions themselves.

Above all, be the person and leader you wish to be. Don't ever compromise your own integrity.

### Integrity shows

*Understanding and Working with Difficult People* and *Me! A Difficult Person?* are the signature books at www.difficultpeople.org. These provide the most comprehensive materials available on working with difficult people. These books and my Work Trilogy: *Succeeding with Difficult Coworkers, Succeeding with Difficult Bosses,* and *Managing Difficult Employees* are also available at major on-line book retailers.

# 64. Competent

Synonyms: capable; able; knowledgeable; experienced; skilled; proficient

Antonyms: incompetent; inept; ineffectual; lacking ability

Competence comes in many forms. Ideally we would like our team and organizational leaders to have a solid knowledge base in a key area of the business before they rise to top management. Most do. In today's business environment it is not unusual for mid-level managers to senior executives to have a wide array of personal, professional, and business expertise that may or may not directly relate to the job they have been given.

Sometimes good leadership comes from the ranks of employees who have a great deal of competence in a specific area and an excellent sense of fundamental leadership. They are promoted along their specific area for a time, and then begin to branch into areas where their expertise is more limited but related. The key is that in the process they are also learning to be competent, quality leaders.

It is important for leaders to have areas of individual accomplishment and competence. It gives them a foundation of knowledge and discipline upon which to build their confidence as a manager and leader. Good leaders also keep on learning.

When an excellent marketing manager gets promoted to Senior vice-president of a plant specializing in production, she may initially feel a bit out of place. But it is highly likely that she was promoted for her abilities not only as a specialist in marketing but as a manager and person who works well with others. Chances are she will succeed and in the process will learn a tremendous amount about production – maybe not the specific technical know-how, but she will learn, because it is in her nature to learn and to expand her horizons.

This book is about competence, in all of its aspects – what it takes not only to be a competent leader, but a good one. Competent people don't become incompetent because they change their emphasis. It is more likely that they will become much more competent. Leaders don't just lead, they learn, grow, and blossom with each new challenge.

Be competent in everything you tackle.

People will notice.

# 65. Discerning

Synonyms: discriminating; astute; shrewd; perceptive; selective

Antonyms: undiscerning; indiscriminate; haphazard; unselective

"Discernment – the ability to find the root of the matter."

(Maxwell, *The 21 Indispensible Qualities of Leadership*)

Discernment takes 'paying attention' to the next level. It is being able to see connections and put things together from everything that we observe. It is a quality of leadership that one develops through careful observation, by being open to possibilities, and by listening.

I also like the word 'perception' or 'being perceptive,' but discernment adds the quality of intelligent judgment or decision-making. Discernment is about making decisions based on information one has gathered. One must weigh various factors and consider various strategies and potential outcomes. Good leaders make the effort to understand as much as possible about a situation or concern before making decisions or passing judgment.

Managers often must make very difficult decisions: decisions about personnel, budget, evaluations and raises, strategies, goal-setting, office dynamics, and so on. Making these decisions requires a leader to weigh many factors. The key qualities needed are integrity, honesty, openness, and concern (caring).

I think the most important idea good leaders need to keep in mind when making any decisions, when they use their powers of discernment, is that whatever they decide and however they make the decision, people are going to be affected. When leaders keep the people they work with at the forefront of their decisions and judgments, they are staying in touch with their own humanity.

Ultimately if you can keep people in the picture, you can't go too far wrong.

# 66. Focus

Synonyms: concentration; attention; attentiveness; mindfulness

Antonyms: inattentive; distracted; unmindful

Focus can be both a positive and negative trait. It is often a matter of balance.

There are times where the ability to focus exclusively on a single matter or concern is needed, and there are other times when a leader needs to be alert and open to many things happening at once.

If I focus so much on one thing, that I tune out everything and everyone else, I may not be taking care of other things that need my attention. However, if I am easily distracted by everything that comes in the door, I may give the impression that I can't give due attention to anything. Leaders have to make choices every day on what to pay attention to and what to focus on.

It is a delicate balance at times and it takes a good bit of wisdom to make the best choices.

Time management is a huge issue for managers in corporations today. Deciding when and how to expend one's efforts are critical decisions. Setting priorities sends clear messages to your employees and coworkers about what is important. If you spend all of your time behind a desk answering e-mails, doing paper-work, and taking phone calls your people are going to wonder how important they are.

My philosophy is that one needs to focus first and foremost on two key areas:

> Things that DIRECTLY impact the organization's/team's vision, i.e. goals of the team and company,
>
> and,
>
> People – Your people.

If you are spending your time on less important matters, regardless of where they come from in the chain of command, you are doing a disservice to yourself and your team members. A great leader knows when to step up and have the courage to tell people above and below in the chain when their 'stuff' is getting in the way of what is most important. Have the courage to tell people what is getting in the way of these two priorities – tell them kindly – but be willing to tell them!

Focus can be learned. As a musician I learned to tune out everything else around me when I was practicing. However, when I was playing in a group, I had to learn not only to focus on what I was doing, but I also needed to be able to hear and react to and communicate with all of the other performers around me. These are skills that are extremely valuable to leadership.

Focus also has more of a global interpretation. Your focus as a leader may be on many things that are perhaps more esoteric:

> You need to have a focus toward the vision of the team you are leading, and toward how that vision melds with and supports the mission of the organization.

> You need to be mindful of how your team is doing from many different perspectives: their productivity; performance; energy; group dynamics, etc.

> It is extremely valuable to be attentive to the work and dynamics of other teams from a line and matrix standpoint, and how they impact your team and your strategies and goals.

> You need to have a feel for the ebb and flow of the entire organization, and how that all fits into the current business climate and global economy.

In this sense focus has to do with awareness and your responsibility as a leader to be open to everything that can impact what your purpose is, and what your team's purpose is within the grand scheme of things. The more you know and stay alert, the better you can make decisions, be discerning, and take care of your people.

# 67. Organized

Synonyms: structured; ordered; prepared

Antonyms: unstructured; free; spontaneous; formless; unplanned

I used to tell my students that there seemed to be two primary divisions to humanity: those people who were organized and those who weren't. Some people just can't seem to get on with life unless everything around them is accounted for and arranged in neat little piles. Others enjoy the freedom of 'letting things go,' letting decisions take care of themselves, and generally going with the flow of things. I always counted myself in the latter group.

Though this limited defining of how the world and the people in it work and play is in some ways accurate, things are never quite so simple.

Leaders need to have the ABILITY to organize. It doesn't necessarily have to be 'who they are.' Leaders don't have to be obsessed with everything being 'just so.' Actually, they probably should avoid rigidity and inflexibility because to succeed in today's business environment of constant change one has to be able to adjust and be able to allow their team players to adjust.

The good leaders I have known personally ranged from people who were almost obsessive about where everything was and how it was done, to those whose offices always looked like a maelstrom had descended. However, all of them were capable of good organization when it was called for and they were also capable of being flexible and supporting innovation.

Structure provides stability and an orientation around which we can build. Some people need us to be very structured for them, while others prefer to be left alone to fend for themselves and they only need us on rare occasions to help them with concerns. In many ways a leader needs to be able to fulfill the needs and address the concerns of his team by providing the structure that is appropriate at any given time and for any given situation.

The focus should be toward using structure as a means to an end, not as the end in itself. If flexibility and creativity are what are needed to move a project forward, then use the talents of the people on your team who fit that approach. If clear data and a concise, well-organized, impeccable report are called for, then make sure there are people on the team who will see that it gets done right.

Knowing your own strengths and weaknesses are important to consider in relationship to structure and organization too.

> I have always tried to hire people who complemented my weaknesses with their strengths. When I write I know that no matter how many times I go through something I will miss things, so I make sure I have careful, scrutinizing people on my review squad. Together we manage to get things done much more precisely than I would by myself.

Much of what we do in a leadership position comes back to how we use our own talents and the talents of others. If we have the right people on the bus, and we have them in the right seats, then our burden of leadership is greatly eased. (See Collins, *Good to Great*) We only have to remember to shift people around when necessary to facilitate the best possible outcome for whatever it is we are tackling. This, to me, is what organization is all about. A leader's job is making sure his/her team has the best organization for the current situation.

Be organized because it serves a purpose –

for you and for your team and organization.

# 68. Engagement

Synonyms: involve; absorb; enlist; mesh

Antonyms: disengage; withdraw


Engagement is

taking a tangible interest in the work of employees...

and getting involved...

to be fully present in every activity you are engaged in.

(Farson and Keyes)


Engagement is a two way street. You want to be engaged in what is happening throughout your work world and you want others to be engaged as well. Interestingly, they are both your responsibility as a leader.

Being engaged is concerned with both paying attention and caring. Not just caring about a product or someone's performance, but in who they are and how they are doing. Leaders who are engaged with their employees concerns have far fewer problems than those that sit by the sidelines guiding and administrating without any true involvement. Managers of this type may be effective managers and administrators, but they are not leaders.

> I have known many managers in my day as an employee and I have listened to them, learned from them in spite of themselves, and put up with them, but they didn't inspire me and I can guarantee that I wouldn't have followed them through hell and back.

> I have also worked for, and with, a few genuine leaders. People who cared and who were engaged with who I was and my concerns and desires. I sometimes did go through what seemed like hell and back for them. (My doctoral work comes to mind.)

Getting fellow workers and employees engaged is another aspect of leadership altogether. I like William Bridges' perspective: To engage people make it their problem; invest them in the solution. (*Managing Transitions*)

If we want people to become involved with, be engaged, in working on something, they need to have ownership. They need to see the rhyme and reason for what they are doing and how they fit into the problem and working toward a solution. They are much more likely to put themselves into something hook, line, and sinker if their heads AND hearts are engaged.

Motivation and inspiration are the result of ownership. Engage yourself and engage others, the payback is enormous.

> "...Our most engaging activities have nothing to do
>
> with winning or losing."
>
> (Farson and Keyes)

# 69. Determined

Synonyms: strong-minded; resolute; firm; unwavering

Antonyms: wavering; hesitant; indecisive

> "'I am persistent in my determination,' she said.
> And, so started the controversy between them
> that has now culminated in the marriage of the century.'"
>
> (Koob, a future novel)

Determination is a mind-set. Persistence is an action. I think great leaders have an aura of determination about them. It manifests in any number of ways, but you see it in how they approach things, the way they talk, and even in their walk. It might come out as stubbornness, which is not an altogether negative trait, or we might see it in the way they tackle a problem with a deliberate kind of focus.

Great leaders are determined to 'Get it Right.'

Perhaps more than any other focus, **Quality** matters a great deal to quality people. If it isn't right, then as my Dad would have said, "By God, you better make it right." There isn't very much, if any, compromise in quality. Good leaders are always looking for a value-added mentality and approach in their team-members. You can always tell an industry, large or small, that really cares about getting it right. It would be interesting to meet the people at the top of these quality-minded industries; just to shake their hands and get a feel for what makes them tick.

As an example:

> I was impressed by the quality of customer service I received on a couple of occasions recently.

I had to call and ask some questions about my new Canon Printer. Not only were they cordial and efficient, they actually had answers and made sure I was satisfied.

Another company that I felt 'Got it Right,' recently was American Airlines: they treated me with courtesy, respect, and compassion far beyond the norm when I needed to change my airplane ticket when my Dad passed away.

Guess what: the Big Name companies that haven't gotten it right in recent memory would probably hate for me to tell their stories! Unfortunately we all have had far too many experiences where companies didn't seem to have any interest in, much less determination to make sure they got things right or satisfied their customers.

Great leaders are also determined to "get it done," but never to the exclusion of "getting it right," in the final analysis. They do foster innovation, experimentation, and even a good bit of risk-taking, in the interest of staying ahead of the competition, but they also insist that the final product or service is top-notch.

We have all been frustrated by the lack of "getting-it-done-ness" in the world today, especially in customer service. I often wonder if executives at companies who have large customer-relation staffs ever actually call up with a problem to see how their system works. If they find themselves shuffled ad infinitum from representative to representative, put on hold for long periods of time, and pretty much all the information they just gave to one representative has to be repeated to the next, would they care enough to make changes? Would they be determined to change things? And just as determined to make sure they got changed?

Great leaders know how well things work in their teams and if they don't work well, they make changes.

Great leaders are determined to be understood and to understand others.

Many leaders are good at "Getting things Done." A fair number are good at "Getting things Right." There are far fewer who seem to be really concerned or determined about making sure that their message, their vision for their team (see Chapter 88), and their Passion are visible. Information is the foundation of our current world (See Gates, *Business @ the Speed of Thought*). As a leader we have to make sure that what we want, care about, do and say, really gets 'out there' and is understood. We have to make priorities VISIBLE! What we spend time on IS what is important, that is how our team members and customers will see us.

We also need to work very hard at understanding others: our team members, our co-managers, people above us in the chain, and our customers and clients. Getting out and being with and talking with people is the ONLY way this can be truly accomplished. Understanding is fundamental to good leadership.

**Be determined about understanding others**

**and what matters to them!**

Great leaders are determined about many things. When something is worth their attention, it is important, and they will find a way to let you know it is important by how they act.

# 70. Energy

Synonyms: vigor; liveliness; get-up-and-go

Antonyms: lifeless; inert; weakness; motionless

Energy implies, for most of us when we apply it to people, a kind of liveliness. "She's energetic." "He's dynamic." Leaders may have this type of energy, but I see their energy as being more of the focused, driven, stick-to-it-tive kind of energy.

I would not typify Winston Churchill or J. F. Kennedy as being energetic, but they certainly seemed to have an amazing drive, founded in what they believed in and what they were striving for.

Energy in the sense of good leadership is more about how leaders get things done. There is a pervasiveness about how they tackle problems and concerns. They have a dogged attitude that shows when they have sunk their teeth into something and are determined to 'get it right.'

One characteristic that I believe typifies great leaders is an amazing amount of energy that is manifested in work-time. While they may not run too many short dashes, they are almost always running marathons. This type of energy is not gender specific either. These are the types of people who could outwork everyone in their group and be ready for more at the end of the day.

Perhaps another characteristic of leadership energy is the ability to find strength when it is needed. Grinding things out day after day is one type of energy; being able to call in reserves when it seems like one can't do anything else is another. The passion and caring of great leaders gives them that burst of energy when they need it most.

Energy in this sense doesn't come from lifting weights and exercising regularly (although that never hurts). It doesn't come from youthful vitality and exuberance.

**It comes from the heart.**

# 71. Down-to-earth

Synonyms: pragmatic; practical; realistic; sensible

Antonyms: flighty; impractical; dreamy

I really like the word 'pragmatic,' unfortunately it is not as well-used and has been recently interpreted rather negatively. Practical and practicality are also good descriptive terms. Whichever word you like to use, I think good leaders have a solid, down-to-earth quality about them. They have no compunction about getting out in the trenches, rolling up their sleeves, and digging into the best and worst of situations. They know what it means to get dirt on their hands and they do it, too, when it is needed.

Pie-in-the-sky desk jockeys have few leadership skills, in my book. If they do not have a fundamental desire to get out there and make a difference where it counts, they don't know how to lead.

Sam Walton comes to mind as a true down-to-earth, practical sort. He knew as well as anyone what it takes to motivate people and to get things done – be practical, be sensible, be out there where you know what is happening.

Good leaders talk to people, too. They use plain language and they know how to get a point across without talking above everyone's heads. They are open and honest because that is how 'plain folks' are. The last words you would use to describe them would be: snobbish, cultured (not because they aren't, but because they don't make a big deal about it); over-bearing; intellectual (Again, not because they aren't smart, but because it is not important to show it off.); and so on.

You might say instead:

> "He's a regular guy."

> "She's just great; she understands what it is like to work here."

"I am glad she pays attention to what we do down here in the lab."

"He's very easy to talk to."

"He's very matter-of-fact, great to work for."

Down-to-earth people make us feel like we matter. They make an effort to understand things from our perspective, not just from an ivory-tower view. When we are with them, we feel like they are just one of the guys/gals regardless of their rank. They don't hold themselves aloof or apart.

Practicality is also about how we approach things. I think great leaders approach the world and their work with a tremendous amount of savvy. They pay attention and bring what they need to any given situation. They never apologize for who they are and what is important to them. However, they are not afraid to apologize when they do mess up.

More than anything else, down-to-earth people are honest.

# 72. Simplicity

Synonyms: ease; straightforwardness

Antonyms: difficulty; complicated; complex

## KIS – Keep It Simple

KISS: Keep It Simple Stupid. I don't believe in self-deprecation, but I do like this acronym, so I tend to shorten it. Simplicity is at the root of good education. One thing I learned many years ago as a student was, 'get the basics right.' If you learn the fundamentals thoroughly the rest will be much, much easier. Learn the simple stuff, the basics, the rest will fall into place.

> I proved this to myself when I was in the United States Air Force Navigator School. My new friend (and now old buddy) and I had been voted (by acclamation) the two most likely to flunk out of Navigator school – because I had majored in violin in college and he had majored in French. The rest of our class members majored in engineering, mathematics, and oher more 'navigator-oriented' subjects.

> Those first three months of navigator school I studied everything they handed me and then some. Not because I was particularly dedicated or a good student, but because I was in love with a girl back in the Midwest and I had nothing better to do. After learning all the basics so well those first three months, I coasted through the next six and graduated second in my class, with my friend not far behind. What I really learned was **how to learn** and how to teach: keep it simple and keep it basic. Learn it right the first time and you will be much more likely to go home with something you won't forget. I teach and try to write with this always in mind.

As a coach one of my challenges is taking what others see as complex and difficult situations (e.g. a situation with a difficult employee), and finding ways to break them down so that everyone can see their way through the concern. When you can step back and analyze almost any situation, it is rarely as difficult, complex, or impossible as you once thought.

Master leaders have this knack – the ability to break down problems and concerns, strategies and goals, evaluation and training, into manageable, understandable parts.

One of the unique aspects of bureaucracy is that it, rather than people, often rule what happens in an organization. Many authors (Peters notably, see *Thriving on Chaos* and other works) emphasize simplifying bureaucratic structures, forms, and procedures. Bill Gates in his book *Business @ the Speed of Thought* recommends putting as many business forms as possible into digital space, e.g. electronic forms simplify use and facilitate measurement as well as eliminate tons of paperwork and storage.

Simplicity takes courage and it takes keeping on top of things. You cannot lead unless you know what is going on. You cannot lead well unless you are willing to listen to what is going on.


### KIS (Keep it Simple)

because when you do, you are being smart, very smart!

# PART VIII
# Free Yourself

# 73. Creativity

Synonyms: originality; ingenuity; resourcefulness

Antonyms: unoriginal; cliché; imitative; uninspired; trite

Creativity is nothing more than using our intellect to find other, more unique, ways of seeing and doing things.

> I usually had one or more students come up to me in my large classes at college and tell me that they couldn't do the creative project I had assigned because they were not creative-types. I would say, "Can you think? Then you can be creative."

We tend to think of creativity in the sense of it being a 'gift' or talent. I don't see it that way. Brainstorming is being creative. Finding a new way to use an old widget is creative. Writing a report is creative, and can be very creative if one has the courage to add a bit of themselves to the project.

**Creativity is**, and you should think about this for at least a minute or two, **more than a little about courage**. It is the courage to take chances as well as the willingness to search inside ourselves and bring out those ideas we all have. You may not feel naturally creative because you haven't used your creativity much or because you have stuffed it (maybe your third grade teacher told you that you weren't creative). Creativity is about having the courage to show others what you are thinking and dreaming.

Good leaders encourage and inspire creativity. In today's business climate where things literally do change "@ the speed of light," (Gates) because of the internet and current technology, it is absolutely necessary to build this into your team's approach. I can think of few, if any, industries that cannot use a good bit of creativity thrown in.

Creativity means taking a look at ideas. It doesn't mean you automatically have to use everything that you dream up, though it is often wise to try new things to see what the possibilities are. (see Chapters 74 through 77, **Innovation**, **Flexibility**, **Experiment**, and **Risk-taking**). It is often about generating ideas that can foster new ways of doing things and new ways of thinking about things.

When a team has the freedom and responsibility to look at things in unique ways, good stuff happens. Post-it Notes (3M) were the result of an experimental failure. It took awhile, but they found an amazing use for a glue that didn't work the way they had originally planned. Somebody got to thinking about what the possibilities might be for this type of mixture rather than flushing it down the proverbial drain. That is creative thinking.

'By the book,' is boring and deadly. Today we have the over-used phrase, 'thinking-outside-the box,' which implies if you can't think outside the box, i.e. creatively, you will fail – and fail to measure up. Good analogy, but creativity is what it is all about.

Creativity is adding some of yourself to what you are working on, not just 'filling-in-the-blanks." The best thing about creativity is that it is fun – and most of us certainly don't have nearly enough fun at work (or maybe in our lives!).

Allowing personnel the freedom to add a bit of themselves to the mix is motivational and it changes the whole atmosphere of how things are done. Everyone from the senior executives to the clerks in the mailroom, the custodians, and the people who load the trucks have ideas and better ways to do things. Good leaders listen and give them wiggle-room. Whenever possible they support, through encouragement and money, ideas that have merit. They take good ideas, give credit to the person or team that generated the idea, and make it happen.

The more you can encourage and support creativity the more vibrant and productive your team will be. There are times when we have to 'follow the book' and fill-in-the-blanks correctly, but there are also many times when flexibility is the only key to innovation.

Creativity is about the freedom to think and do. Set yourself and your team free. You might be surprised, very pleasantly surprised, at what happens next.

# 74. Innovation

Synonyms: novelty; improvement; progress; development

Antonyms: hackneyed; stale; tired; unoriginal

Innovation is now. It is something that businesses over the past few decades have come to realize is an essential aspect of economic life in our world today. Companies, even the large old masters of bygone decades, cannot afford to rely on their old products and old ways of doing things. The global economy is growing at an exponential rate and challenges and competition will be coming from sources we would never have imagined ten years ago.

> "Measure (and reward) the future – not the past."
>
> (Gerstner)

From creative thinking comes the potential for innovation. Companies and leaders need to encourage the development and experimentation of new ideas just to stay up with the competition. Innovation has to become a major thrust of time, energy, and money spent, if businesses are to succeed today.

Change has become such a constant in the business world that leaders need to begin to recognize it not as something that gets in their way and causes problems, but as something positive – a catalyst for innovation and growth. Opportunities abound during times of change, and getting your people involved and excited about new ways of doing things and new ways of thinking is a positive perspective in an otherwise disruptive time. Get them up and get them moving, and then they will become involved in the process. They will start finding solutions rather than wallowing in 'what used to be.'

Innovation and creative thinking are natural ways of life for some team members. Others may be more inclined to prefer the stability of tried and true methods of thinking and doing. Farson and Keyes have a unique perspective,

"Keep those who aren't innovative

out of the way of those who are."

(*Whoever Makes the Most Mistakes Wins*)

In part I agree with this statement, because innovative people need to have the freedom and support to do what they do best. In another sense, I think innovative personnel can help motivate and encourage those who tend to stick to the way things have always been done. They can help them become more forward-thinking. Good leaders make the best use of the talent and style of their personnel without anyone feeling pushed too strongly out of their comfort zone.

Sometimes innovation is using things in new ways, looking at something a bit differently than before; and sometimes it is out and out doing something completely different. As a leader you have to be willing to open the doors wide enough for people to feel they can take the bull by the horns and run with ideas. The leader serves as a guide, supporter, interference blocker, and cheerleader. Her talents need to be utilized in making appropriate, informed decisions about what, when, if, where, and how things are pursued, while at the same time juggling the feelings of those who are bringing new ideas to the table.

Innovation is crucial to business success today, but it also needs to be intelligently guided. Responsibility and freedom are earned through effort, failure, and success. Structure and organization can be part of the whole process of innovation in a team or organization. It is the leader who sets the guidelines and parameters for success.

# 75. Flexibility

Synonyms: elasticity; suppleness

Antonyms: rigid; unyielding; severe; inflexible; unbending

There is no doubt that great leaders often have a stubborn streak. They can dig their feet into the ground and ride out the most serious challenges to their own ideas and decisions. But they can also be tremendously flexible when necessary and more importantly, they can recognize when it is judicious to be more open to change.

Evard and Gipple have an interesting list in *Managing Business Change for Dummies*. I will expand on their thoughts briefly.

Flexible individuals:

"Don't get derailed...by unseen circumstances"

> In other words they keep an open mind and can see opportunity in changing times. Leaders react to change by finding new ways to motivate their teams and by helping them find solutions to concerns.

"Know that (all) situations contain both positive and negative elements"

> A great way to look at the world and its challenges is "What can I do about this." (Accepting a challenge) Rather than, "What am I going to do about this." (Woe is me.) One is proactive, the other is reactive. This is how coaches look at the world and how they work with others. Great leaders look at things with the mind-set of, "Here is a challenge; what can we do about it? What can we learn from the process of dealing with it." Some of the best training and education comes when we encounter and learn from difficulties we have to deal with.

"Don't expect events or people to be predictable"

> Life is rarely predictable and one always has to maintain flexibility in order to deal with whatever comes up. A good leader will build into any program or project the ability to change directions and make adjustments as needed. He will also encourage his team to have the same attitude and approach. "Be prepared," is a good slogan for leaders to follow, too.

"Accept(s) the fluidness and impermanence of life"

> I like the term 'fluidness' or 'fluidity.' (See Chapter 78). Keeping our eyes and ears open to everything around us allows us to 'go with the flow.' It is amazing how many serendipitous things happen when we stay alert to the possibilities and have the freedom to make adjustments when opportunities present themselves.

"Are comfortable with the diversity of others' opinions and operating styles"

> Differences are the most common cause of angst between people (difficult people.org).

> Understanding this and working with differences can solve many concerns before they exist or become exacerbated. How we and others do things or think about things can be vastly different. Great leaders learn to use these differences between people to build strong productive teams. Rather than forcing people to fit a mold of what is 'the right way of doing things,' they mold solutions around their people's interests and strengths.

"Are not tied to one way of doing things"

> Some people like the stability of the tried and true. It is a luxury that most leaders cannot afford, especially today. Decisions need to be made based on what is best, not just

on what worked before. Leaders build some flexibility into everything they do and it is always a part of their leadership style and approach. They stay open to the possibilities at every turn.

"Can see problems from many perspectives"

This is a coaching skill and one that wise managers build into their repertoire as much as possible. Taking a step back and considering differing perspectives, often brought out by different team members, is a valuable tool in a solution-oriented organization. Leaders can move people away from 'being right' to thinking about what is best. It is an important delineation.

Being flexible is not always easy. We are all set in our ways, to a certain extent. Typically the more we live and work on this earth, the more we like to do things in a certain way. Staying on top of what we add to the equation in the sense of openness and flexibility is a very important leadership skill. Stay alert, pay attention, and be willing to move when you need to and be willing and able to help others move, too.

# 76. Experiment

Synonyms: research; test; trial; try out

Antonyms: stay the same; remain as is

"Experiment a Little Every Day (Starting Today)"

(Bridges, *Managing Transitions*)

Experimentation is taking our creativity and quest for innovation to the next level. We try things out. The important part of this concept for leaders is that this doesn't necessarily mean a massive experimental process that will take years, tons of money, and involve lots of people.

Experimentation at its best is grassroots, starts modestly, and grows from small successes.

Encourage trials at every level. Support that youngster who has a keen mind and maybe that just a bit over-the-top crazy idea. Often real grassroots experimentation costs very little, is motivational, and even if it doesn't bring out the next Velcro, it might stir some other ideas, new ways of using old products, or new experiments that do go someplace.

The whole concept of experimentation is that it is okay to try something out and fail. Or better yet it is GOOD to try things out, even if we fail, because we learn much more from our failures, typically, than from our successes. Farson and Keyes state, "Managers can do much to convert an employee's sense of failure into one of experimentation, learning, and growth." I would take this a step further and say that one of the key responsibilities of a leader is to help his team members see errors and failures as a means of improving and learning. Otherwise experimentation will never have the legs to get anything off the drawing table.

A wise manager budgets for things that 'just come along.' They know, too, that great ideas come from all sorts of folk.

As a teacher for many years, I have always taken one concept with me wherever I have been and it has always paid off – there is something that can be learned from everyone – the good teachers, the bad teachers, and the average-everyday-type teachers.

Sometimes what we learn by paying attention and trying new things out is what won't work and how not to do things. These all give us more data for the next time we try something. I have learned some of my most valuable work and life lessons from the very worst managerial examples and also from my own worst screw-ups. Give people a chance to be heard. Some of the silliest ideas may have something in them that lights your team's fire and sets them off in a new direction.

William Bridges has an interesting perspective:

When someone says that something can't be done.

Ask "Why not?"

(*Managing Transitions*)

You might want to follow "Why not?" with a challenge to them and your team, "Let's see whether we can make this work." People like challenges and even small ones can really get people going.

All good leaders have questioning attitudes. When an obstacle gets in their way, they seek solutions and they enervate people to find ways to solve things. Great leaders have an attitude when it comes to obstacles that is nothing less than dogged. I think they actually enjoy the challenges of finding ways around something that gets in their way. (see Chapter 69, "**Determined**.")

The pharmaceutical industry is an excellent example of experimentation at work. If it wasn't for hundreds and thousands of failed trial and error attempts from the beginning chemical structures through molecular experimentation to animal and clinical trials, we wouldn't have drugs like the latest antibiotics, pain-killers and anti-inflammatory drugs, AIDS and cancer drugs, etc.

Trial and error are how we learn. Watch any young child attempting to do something for the first time.

Experimentation is how we succeed, one failed attempt at a time.

# 77. Risk-taking

Synonyms: adventuresome; exciting; daring

Antonyms: cowardly; unadventurous; unexciting; tedious

"The biggest regrets in life are for risks we didn't take,
not for ones we took and lost."

(Farson and Keyes)

"A man's life is interesting primarily when he has failed...
For it is a sign that he tried to surpass himself."

(Georges Clemenceau)

Many of the management and change books I have been reading emphasize the importance of taking risks and making mistakes. (Peters; Farson and Keyes, and others) There is almost no room in the business world today for people who aren't willing to take chances. Status quo, complacency, the same ol' stuff, just don't hack it anymore. The world is changing too rapidly and you can be assured that your neighbor halfway across the globe, is doing everything he can to get ahead of you.

We all question taking risks: "What will my boss think?" "Maybe it won't work out;" "I won't be good enough;." "I'll get fired;" "I'll look bad;" "I hate to lose;" "I feel bad when I do something dumb, wrong, or make a mistake;" etc. Taking risks creates anxiety and stress, but it can also create excitement and energy. It is all in how you approach it.

The truth is that risk takers – people who fail more than they succeed, who take chances – make the most impact in their fields.

> Thinking back on my life, the times I have stepped up to the plate and swung have been far more interesting than

the times I have not, and almost invariably, with very few exceptions, I have not regretted the swing – even if I missed, and missed, and missed again. Why? Because we learn from our mistakes and somewhere down the road we are going to hit the ball, maybe even a home run, because we were willing to take that first swing, and the next, and the next...

Tom Peters uses a quote from the hockey player, Wayne Gretzky,, in his book *The Circle of Innovation*:

"You miss 100 percent of the shots you don't take."

It is a great way to look at why taking risks is not really all that risky.

Encouraging experimentation, innovation, **taking risks** can be risky. But it can also pay off in many ways.

It is motivational if you support your personnel through failures and successes

It raises the bar for everyone, and it is fun.

You are guaranteed to learn something.

It is fairly likely that you will be building your team in the process.

Calculated risks? Certainly. Whenever feasible, gathering as much information as possible is smart business. Good information can reduce the risks you are taking exponentially, but there are never one hundred percent guarantees for anything. There is also a balance between taking too much time to gather information and the point at which you are willing to jump into the fray. There typically isn't much tentativeness in leaders who make a difference. They learn what they can as quickly as they can and then they decide.

Leaders encourage risk-taking by being proactive about creativity, innovation, and experimentation. They support risk-takers by allowing plenty of leeway for those who are taking intelligent, well-researched risks that are coupled with good old-fashioned hard work. And they treat failures as bumps in the road that are to be learned from and used as the catalyst for new efforts.

Supporting those who are willing to take risks takes wise management. Some people are extraordinary creative thinkers, but have difficulty with implementation. Some are great planners and strategists, but lack the production and technical know-how to bring a plan to fruition. Good leaders build teams that can make the most of the combined talents needed to bring a project to life and see it through at least the early experimentation phase. As success builds, the project team can be expanded to include all those who are needed to see the gambit through to full production and marketing.

Then there is that thing called intuition – sometimes you just have to go with a gut feeling and stick your neck out a bit further than is comfortable. Just don't forget to use your head in the process.

Take a chance, Steve Brodie did.

(See Chapter 79)

# 78. Fluidity

Synonyms: smoothness; effortlessness; facility; ease

Antonyms: awkward; unstable; difficulty

> "Only systems that evolve continually can compete
>
> in a constantly changing economy."
>
> (Farson and Keyes)

Fluidity is a great descriptive word. Far too often our life is anything but fluid, especially our work life. There are constant stresses over work, worry, deadlines, difficult people and difficult situations we must deal with every day, and on and on. Take a look at one of your typical work weeks and add them all up. Be forewarned, it might be a depressing exercise, unless...

...unless at some point you make a decision to just 'go with the flow.'

I spent a major portion of my life up until a few years ago fighting a mighty but losing battle with many of those things in that list above and then some.

**What did I gain?**

Headaches, backaches, spirit-aches, and negativity.

**What did I lose?**

Sleep, peace of mind, my health, and positivity.

But I was right! And THEY were wrong.

Finally I chose to allow a bit of flow into my life.

**What did I have to give up?**

Being right.

**What did I have to do?**

Open my eyes.

What is so all fired important about being right that we set ourselves up for all kinds of stress, anxiety, and illness as a result? Do we fear that we will lose our manhood or womanhood if we are wrong or if we don't fight all these needless battles?

Letting your life be more fluid is simply taking a different perspective of things. Instead of being right all the time, find ways to be kind and find ways for everyone to be right.

> Sound familiar: It used to end up that we all were right, and we were all wrong at the same time. And nobody was happy because no one would give in.

Instead of worrying about everything that might happen, keep your eyes and ears open to what IS happening and deal with stuff, now!

'Might haves' and 'might have beens' serve us no purpose except to feed our egos. Instead of seeing difficulties as big pains, see them as challenges that can be learned from. Instead of seeing difficult people as being difficult, make the effort to understand who they are and why they are the way they are. Many times that kind of attention is all that is needed for them to be 'less difficult' anyway.

We can look at the world from a wide variety of perspectives. Thinking about choosing your battles wisely and letting the rest of life flow around you while you pay attention to it, rather than constantly bucking it, is an amazing transformation. Life and work suddenly open up completely new vistas for you.

You will learn more, have a more positive impact on others, and have more fun, too.

# 79. Chances

Synonyms: risks; gambles; ventures; tries

Antonyms: quits; won't risk


Here is a great question to ask yourself every day,

> "What totally outrageous thing would you do
>
> if the outcome was guaranteed?"
>
> (Lunden)


If we could guarantee results we would probably all be willing to take more chances.

Calculated risk-taking is smart business, but sometimes YOU just have to take chances.

I am in awe of some mid-level managers (associate directors, senior directors, vice-presidents) I have met. They are highly intelligent, masters in a given field of study, honest, all about quality, and passionate about what they do. They are exemplars for what a good leader should be, EXCEPT, unfortunately, they are also scared. They seem afraid to go up against the 'big boys and girls' even when it is something that they passionately believe in, something that needs to be done differently. OR, if they are willing at times to make some waves, they do it through some backhanded, or less than forthright manner that invariably fails because there was no conviction behind their effort and nobody understood how importantly they really felt about it.


Take a chance;

Steve Brodie did.

I studied with a great teacher at the University of Illinois while working on my Doctoral Degree, Dr. Charles Leonhard. 'Charlie' often told the story about Steve Brodie, the first person to jump off the Brooklyn Bridge (1886) and live to tell about it. Brodie became famous because of his stunt. He opened a popular tourist bar in the Bowery section of New York City and made the most of his supposed exploit. There was even a long-running play that he appeared in about the stunt.

Whether Steve Brodie did jump off the bridge is debatable, but he became famous because people thought he did. Evidence suggests he may have had a dummy thrown off the bridge and then he leapt from a support much lower down and was pulled aboard a ferry. The point, however, isn't to go jumping off a big bridge. (Please don't!) It is the willingness to make something of yourself and go after what you believe in. The biggest chance Steve Brodie took was with his reputation, not his life.

Charlie's point was that if we want to really make something of our lives we have to take chances.

Taking chances is somewhat different from your standard risk-taking. Sometimes you have to swallow hard and decide to do what is uncomfortable though it may put your reputation and job on the line. [Interestingly enough, this is rarely the case, even though it may feel that way.]

If you believe that things aren't being done right and that your team or organization is struggling to produce a quality product because of bureaucratic nonsense, you have two basic initial choices: make changes; or don't – and be frustrated). Takes courage? Take guts? You bet, especially the first few times.

Taking chances can mean "Just doing it." And sometimes that is the best approach.

There are often times during the change process when we have decisions to make, sometimes very difficult decisions. Sometimes we just have to take the plunge and forge ahead by being willing to take a chance on something. You may feel safer not moving, but it is not much fun, and you don't go anywhere.

If you want a safer approach to things, broach your ideas with the powers that be. Be willing to get everything together and ready to go before taking it forward. Unfortunately, many managers fail when they try to do this because they do not bring passion and conviction to the table with them. If you really want to push through an agenda, you need to be direct, open, and honest about what you want to do. There can be no form of hesitation, suggesting, 'sort-ofs,' 'maybes,' and 'I wannas.'

Just DO IT!

And,

SAY IT!

"I feel very strongly about changing the way we do 'x.' I know traditionally we have done 'y,' but I would like to lay out my plan and show you why I think this method is better. Take a look at this..."

If you have all your ducks in a row, chances are even if you get 'No' for an answer, you will have impressed your boss with how you went about it. Much of the time, and I truly believe this from both my personal experience and professional coaching experience, you will get somewhere and you will open many eyes to what you are all about and who you are as a leader and as a person. Most people are receptive to new ideas. How you broach them is absolutely key. If you hesitate, you have lost before you began. Be positive, open, and passionate about what you believe in and bring that to the table.

Very rarely are you actually putting your job or reputation on the line. If anything, you should look better to the powers-that-be for having had the chutzpah to make the effort. Yes, you should think this through, but not to the point where you discourage yourself. And yes, you need to have a good feel for the person or group you will be presenting this to.

**GET OUT THERE AND TAKE SOME CHANCES!**

Your (our) world is not going to change significantly unless you do. AND we need people who are willing to change the world. We need people in the business world who are having more fun, too!

# 80. Imagination

Synonyms: imagery; resourcefulness; vision; envision; mind; thoughts; creativity

Antonyms: practical; matter-of-fact; staid

Imagination is essentially thinking about things in new ways, and it is closely aligned with creativity. The significance of the word at this point in this book is our willingness as leaders to encourage 'new thinking' in our team members. Most importantly it is encouraging them to use their imaginations every day, in and with everything they do.

All too often we all get into ruts – the same ol', same ol' routine. Boredom sets in. People get complacent. Suddenly the energy and productivity are slipping.

Every person on your team and every person on the periphery of your team has an impact on what you do and they all probably have ideas about things every day. It could be something as simple and basic as, "Why don't we get a container to dispense cotton swabs for each of the lab tables so that we don't have to leave them lying around (unsanitary and possibly a scientifically unsound practice) or have to run to the cabinet every five minutes," or it could be much more monumental, like changing the fundamental design for a new computer chip.

Great ideas often come in strange ways at the very oddest of times. You are not going to be able to take advantage of these serendipitous moments unless you are alert to the possibility and you are never going to hear most of them unless you encourage people to open up and tell you what they are thinking about.

One approach is to have sessions where everyone just throws out ideas, i.e. brainstorming sessions, but with an important rule attached – There is no evaluation involved, period.

People talk, people listen

People ask questions to seek clarification

People support

If there is to be value placed on the ideas that are generated, it will come later. Let people offer what they have. With this type of process, ideas, even crazy ideas, can be recognized and can add value.

Value is added because people are tossing around many things that might jog other ideas.

Value is added because people open up and are willing to take chances.

Value is added because people are motivated.

Value is added because people get involved with each other (team building).

Value is added because the process is positive and open.

And so on.

**Use your imagination!**

**Help and encourage others to use theirs!**

# 81. Friction-free

Synonyms: ease; easiness; smoothness; no difficulty

Antonyms: friction; resistance; abrasion

This is great phraseology. I think this has been around for awhile, as I have run into it several times recently, but I will give credit to the first source – It was a major point made at a conference I attended in Toronto led by the late Thomas Leonard, founder of Coachville.

This is one of those stick on the refrigerator or tape-it-to-the-computer items. If it hasn't been overused in your organization, get some signs up or throw it out there for thought and discussion.

Wouldn't it be great if we could make everything in our lives and work 'friction-free?'

To me the important thing about this idea is just thinking about this and how we might use it to impact what we do. This ties in with the chapter above on imagination, but focuses us toward freeing up our environment and work life. We all enjoy life more when we find easier ways to do things.

There are many little irritations that frustrate us at work every day. When we pay attention to them and bring these frustrations to light we can find ways to change things. We all talk about bureaucracy. We all have our little complaints. We all tend to resign ourselves to living with them.

Why?

Why complain, blame, and wallow in our frustrations? Be solution-focused and find answers! Friction-free doesn't mean the world is suddenly going to be easy for you. It means you are going to find ways to make your world a better, smoother-functioning place for yourself and others.

Take a chance and make the effort to create a more friction-free work space and a more friction-free life. Take a chance and make some changes. Take a chance and talk to people proactively rather than 'inactively' or 'retroactively.' DO SOMETHING!

As a leader take a small chance and talk this up. When people have the space and opportunity to change things and feel they are at the very least listened to, individual and group dynamics change. We feel more in-control and active. We can turn from complaining and criticizing to being solution-oriented.

Friction-free means making things easier. We all do it naturally within our own space and the areas in which we feel we are free and in control. When we expand the concept to include our entire work space and everything that impacts us and our team at work – WOW! (See Chapter 94, "**Zesty**")

**Help create a friction-free mentality at work**

# 82. Anticipates

Synonyms: expect; foresee; predict; do in advance

Antonyms: waits; lags; pauses; delays; holds up

Being on top of things is probably a consistent goal of every leader. It just tends to be much harder to accomplish in real life. We get overloaded and swamped by so many things, so many decisions, that it seems impossible just to keep our head above water from one minute to the next. Who has time to stay ahead of the game? You do, if you want to get ahead. It is often about making choices (see Chapter 86).

However, good leaders do manage to anticipate many things. It is one of those characteristics that make a difference. So what gives them the edge?

Listening

Paying attention/staying alert

    To themselves

    To others

    To the energy and dynamics of their team(s)

    To quality

Communicating clearly and effectively

Taking chances

Being open to innovation and new ideas

Making decisions quickly and efficiently when they need to

Facilitating what others do

Most importantly, they believe in themselves and what they are doing.

Being able to anticipate and stay ahead of the game does have a lot to do with our self-worth and self-confidence. Too often people lose their edge because they begin to be afraid of making choices. They are afraid of what will happen and what will happen to them. I often ask executives I coach, "What is more important, being happy or being cautious?"

"But..."

There are no 'buts'. 'Buts' are excuses you live with for the rest of your life.

Excuses are about fear and not facing that fear. When we face the concerns we have and really take a good look at what we are feeling, most of them vanish into the woodwork. Finally and ultimately being able to anticipate is about knowing ourselves, knowing others, and knowing what is important.

# 83. Facilitates

Synonyms: helps to happen; aid; assist; help

Antonym: Impede; obstruct; hinder; hamper

Leaders make things happen. They make things happen by helping others to make things happen.

This is one of the most important responsibilities of leadership – being willing and able to facilitate the success of others.

There is no room in true leadership for jealousy, in-fighting, one-up-manship, beating others to the punch, etc. Those are all ego-driven, self-righteous behaviors. There is certainly nothing wrong with striving to get ahead, but when it is at the expense of others there is something terribly wrong.

Being willing to stand up for what one believes in is one way we facilitate our work. Another way is by standing up for what our team members believe in and are striving for. There is very little that seems worse in my mind than the leader who encourages, fosters, develops and then doesn't have what it takes to bring things to the next level when he/she runs into an obstacle. Whether it is bureaucracy, individual stubbornness, unexpected crises, forced changes, or other difficulties, a leader needs to be willing to make an effort, sometimes an all-out effort, to get things done, to get things rolling again.

It does take courage. It often takes a willingness to take some risks. But more than anything else it takes caring. People notice when you try to do things for them, for your group, for yours' and your team's vision – not half-hearted attempts, but real effort. True teamwork comes from the willingness of all players to help each other. So leadership also includes the ability to facilitate others facilitating each other.

When the wheel is being greased on a regular basis, things happen, and they tend to happen at a much faster pace. The more we help others to do what they do, the easier our job becomes, too. When a leader doesn't have time for his players and their concerns, he is wasting his own time.

This is a hard concept to get across to many managers. They always have excuses as to why they don't get out in the trenches and talk to people, why they don't follow-up with ideas, why they don't pay attention to the nitty-gritty of what is happening in their groups. Then they wonder why things get bogged down, and why they have all these concerns.

Time spent with your people is never wasted. NEVER! If you feel you are wasting your time, you aren't keeping your eyes and ears open and you are not open to the possibilities. Get out of the leadership game, because you don't belong.

**Facilitating is leading.**

**Leading is facilitating.**

Get it right. Or get out!

# 84. Curiosity

Synonyms: inquisitiveness; interest; nosiness

Antonyms: apathy; indifference; lack of interest


Curiosity might have killed the cat, but I bet she enjoyed herself right up until the end.

Curiosity is the foundation for this section (Part VIII: FREE Yourself!). If you are not curious, you miss out on a lot of life. If your team isn't curious, they are missing out on many opportunities.

> I don't know, but I was either born with an innate inquisitiveness or I got it somehow from my parents. I was one of those inveterate question-askers and I will bet, though I don't really remember, that I drove my teachers and the nuns in my religion classes batty.

Curiosity is about asking:

## Why?

"Why can't we?" is a great question for leaders to use a lot.

## How?

Talk about getting people on board. Most people love this challenge if they have enough space and the freedom to go get the answer.

## When?

Things always have a time component. Get people on top of that right away and get them to stick to their guns or tell you why they didn't.

**Where?**

Got space? Got enough freedom? Get it done!

**How much?**

We can't get away from that money thing, but you can get lots of ideas for how to keep the budget down if you just ask. Good managers learn to scrounge for things.

**Who?**

You might be surprised, very surprised, at who wants to jump on the bandwagon – if you are willing to ask.

**What?**

What, what? There are hosts of 'whats.' It is the best curiosity question there is. Just be prepared to listen.


Curiosity is about seeking. It is not necessary to always come up with answers. The seeking part often tells us much more than we ever anticipated. We have fun in the process. We learn a lot. We get better.

Be curious about the world. Be curious about the world you work in. Be curious about the people you work with. [There is a propriety limit, but most people like you to take an interest in them and their work.]


Be curious about everything…


Curious, isn't it?

# 85. Initiative

Synonyms: inventiveness; enterprise; ingenuity; forward

Antonyms: hesitant; diffident; reserved; reticent

Boom! There he goes taking chances again.

Leaders have tremendous initiative. They do, and they motivate to do. They get things done, always, and they get more things done when it really counts (when their world and the world of their fellows is in turmoil).

> I am reminded of Patton's volunteering his Army to relieve the beleaguered 101$^{st}$ during the Battle of the Bulge. He took initiative and he and his team members got it done.

One of the characteristics of true leadership is being able to rise to the occasion when it is necessary. It is not that leaders don't show initiative on a daily basis, but we often see what this really means when there is a crisis.

9-11 brought out an amazing amount of quality leadership. That horrible day showed this country and its citizens what leadership and initiative are all about. From firefighters to policeman to Mayor Guiliani and Governor Pataki to our President, to our citizens, people took the initiative and MOVED. They made decisions and did things because it was right and it was needed. They rose to that occasion.

Initiative is something that we use on a daily basis, and it is something we rely on when things get tough. It is about making decisions, taking risks sometimes, and making choices. It is also about helping others make choices, too.

When I think of this word, I think of 'being first,' 'starting,' i.e. 'initiating.' You don't wait for others to help make up your mind, you get going. Initiative has to do with those times when time does

matter; when we need to make choices without a great deal of planning, strategizing, and contemplation. We **do**...things. We don't...'just sit around twiddling our thumbs.' [Another of my dad's great expressions.]

In the business world of today, where things can change very rapidly, it takes leaders with initiative (and the foresight to be that way) to stay ahead of the game. Leaders sometimes have to make decisions without having all the facts and even without spending time weighing all the possibilities. When you can, certainly do so, but also be willing to take a chance and make a leap when it is needed.

# 86. Choices

Synonyms: options; alternatives; unlimited

Antonyms: no options; limited; restricted; narrow

We all make choices every day. Leaders make lots of choices every day that affect a lot of people. How can we make wise choices? How can we live up to what is expected of us by the choices we make?

I look at the coaching profession as a profession that helps people see the wide array of choices they have so they CAN make wise, informed decisions. Leaders in many ways need to learn to be coaches. Great leaders are.

So often in life we find ourselves blocked into corners. No matter how we think and worry about a problem, there doesn't seem to be any good way out. The truth is there are probably many choices and many ways out. We just can't see them from our blinders-on perspective.

Worry, frustration, and crises narrow our vision. We allow ourselves to be so wrapped up in something emotionally that it is very difficult to step back and make logical decisions. Making wise choices in difficult situations is often about being able to take a step back emotionally and see things from a detached standpoint.

It is not that we should ignore our emotions, because they have validity, and our feelings can help us make better decisions.

For example: fear can get us alert when danger threatens; sadness tells us we need to grieve, etc.

What it IS about is observing what our emotions are and how they are impacting our ability to make a decision. That brief moment in which we are able to observe ourselves, what we are feeling and what we are thinking, gives us the chance to see other options:

> If I am upset about something someone said to me that is deprecatory, I may react with a sudden retort or defensive

remark. When I take a small 'step back' to observe my feelings and thoughts, I can choose to respond in the same way or make a more positive choice for myself in this particular situation.

I have used a technique that I learned about while working at the VA Medical Center in San Diego under Dr. John McQuaid's tutelage. John came up with a simple mnemonic device that I have found very helpful and easy to use: "**Catch it; Check it; Change it**," "**The Three 'C's**.'" It has to do with observing our own emotions, thoughts, and reactions in stressful situations – times when we need to be able to make wise choices.

"**Catch it**," means to take a step back and simply observe what you are thinking and feeling. It is the best way I know to get out of circuitous thinking and worry. You can do it instantaneously in your head or, as I have found useful if it is something I am perseverating about, I write my feelings and thoughts down on paper. I have found nothing better if I am locked into a worry-cycle, than getting my thoughts and feelings down on paper and seeing them in hard copy. Suddenly it all seems to get much clearer.

"I am stressing here."

"I am worried."

"I am going over the same ground again and again."

"I feel awful."

And so on

The second step, "**Check it**," refers to looking at what you are thinking and feeling and assessing it in whatever ways you can and as specifically as you can. For instance,

"I am feeling anxious, my shoulder muscles are tight, I feel nauseous, and I am afraid of making a decision and what might happen if I do. I am thinking that..."

"These are my choices as I see them, and this is what might happen if..."

And so on.

The difference in what you were probably doing before and using this technique is that you are looking at things from a step removed. It is no longer, 'God, this is awful. I feel terrible. I don't know what to do. The world is going to cave in. If I do this, I'll lose my job for sure," etc. You are making other choices already by simply observing and acknowledging what you are going through. You are maintaining more control of yourself and the situation.

The third step is the choices part: "**Change it**." You arrive at a point where you can make a better choice. Or at least you have the option to make other choices. Instead of the typical circle of reacting and worry that result from your thoughts and feelings, you have stopped and looked. You are more aware and often, as a result, you see that you have more choices or that the choices you have to make are not as bad as you thought.

The words, "Choose wisely," have become sort of a slogan at difficultpeople.org. They are part of one of our sayings: "Negativity breeds Negativity; Positivity breeds Positivity; Choose wisely," and they often crop up at the ends of other statements too. They serve to remind us that we have control if we want it. We can only choose wisely when we are in-control (see **Self-Control**, Chapter 8). This little "**Catch it; Check it; Change it**" technique can help you to choose wisely!

Living in fear of choices we have to make wastes time, energy, and makes us less effective as a leader and as a person.

Some people become almost immobilized by this type of fear. Sometimes as a leader we have to work with others to help them make choices, too. The little device above coupled with an atmosphere of openness and acceptance can do wonders in helping others move ahead and in helping them remain motivated.

We all make mistakes and make poor choices at times. It is part of learning and part of life. Supporting people through the choices they make means allowing them some room to make mistakes as long as we also help them learn from their mistakes and help them to make better choices next time.

Life would be pretty boring if we didn't have choices to make. With a little effort we can expand the horizons when we and others do have to make important choices. It helps us choose wisely!

# PART IX

## Live Life Out Loud

### (Emile Zola and Thomas Peters)

This is a great perspective!

I want to live as many moments of my life
**OUT LOUD** as possible.

It is my choice!

When we are troubled, frustrated, worried, ill, or just plain down, we lose sight of making the most of this day, this moment in time. Taking a small step back and re-examining our concerns with this "go get 'em attitude,' can help. When we are honest about our feelings and thoughts, even if they aren't what is acceptable or even if we don't necessarily like how we feel, at least we now can DO SOMETHING. We can open the bucket of worms, (Cans are too small, we need a <u>bucket</u> of worms here.) and deal with it in some way. We can wade into the challenges that face us.

None of us is perfect. We all have our failings and our concerns and problems. Where we get into the most trouble is when we can't admit them to ourselves and to the people we care about. Today I think living life out loud means I need to be honest about who I am, how I feel, and how I can deal with that to the best of my ability.

Tomorrow it may mean something new, and different, and exciting, too.

# 87. Passion

Synonyms: ardor; excitement; enthusiasm; zeal

Antonyms: boredom; tedium; world-weariness; tiresomeness

"Got Heart?"

"Got Heart" about your work?

When we have passion about what we do we put so much more into it – so much more of ourselves. Passionate people make great employees.

"Got Heart" about the people you work with?

Do you really care about how the people you work with succeed, feel, develop?

How do you manifest that on a <u>daily</u> basis?

Having heart about people is what motivation is all about. Got Heart about ALL the people you work with – colleagues, boss, assistants, etc? You should. They are all people. They are all people who impact your world almost every day.

"Got Heart" about yourself?

If you don't – you are probably not having much fun and you may just be missing one of the most important reasons for your being here on this earth. Have passion about yourself and EVERYTHING you do. It will rub off, BIG-time.

I also like Tom Peters and Nancy Austin's take:

"Courage and self-respect are the lion's share of passion.

Passion opens you to criticism, disappointment,

disillusionment and failure,

any one of which is enough to scare off the bravest of souls."

(*A Passion for Excellence*)

But it is worth it!

The truth is if what you are producing doesn't have any soul, it is not worth much. Not to you, and probably not to your team members.

There is always my mantra,

"If you are not having fun, something's wrong."

If you are not passionate about your work, you are probably not having much fun – adjust. Please. Because so much of our lives are spent at work and we bring so much of our work life home with us.

Find your passion – it is there, you may have to do a little digging, and you will certainly have to make some adjustments.

Be full of heart about yourself and what you do.

It is the only way you can be full of heart for others.

# 88. Vision

Synonyms: mental picture; image; dream; imagination

Antonyms: practical; down-to-earth


There has been a tremendous amount written about vision in the business world. My intention is not to talk about how to get a vision, but to discuss it in terms that are more close to home than an organizational vision.

Vision at all levels should be something we can buy into and feel good about. The global vision for a major company probably makes sense, hopefully elicits some nods and agreement, and may, when we really think about it, offer some inspiration. Global visions for companies are important, but they are also often a bit 'out there,' i.e. something that we all are aware of and is in the back of our minds, but doesn't quite kick us into gear every day when we head for work.

A leader needs to ask this question:


> What can kick me and my team members into gear on a daily basis?


Leaders need to have a personal vision and they need to help their team(s) have a vision that is more personal and inspirational for what they do every day. Yes, these 'inner visions' should meld with the more global image that a corporation has, but they are more intimate. They are something we can relate to immediately and often.

I feel very strongly that a leader needs to have a personal vision. It doesn't necessarily need to be something that we put down on paper, but it should be something that we really believe in and want to live up to on a day to day, moment to moment basis. It can be simple, "Integrity, Ownership, Service." Or it can something more involved, like a list of values or truths we hold close. It should be terse and something you can reflect on instantaneously.

My personal work vision is "Service." While there are many other things I could include and that impact my work, this is my focus – I want to be of service to others.

Personal vision gives us direction. My vision focuses me on making sure that everything I write and do has service to others as an integral component. I don't forget about all the other things that are important to who I am and what my work is about, but I make sure of this one.

Team visions are also important. They need to be personal to the extent that every team member feels that the vision applies to them and what they do on a daily basis. It doesn't work well if it is some esoteric, long-winded doctrine that is worth considering once a year when someone puts it into a speech. I think it is also advisable to stay as much as possible away from formal and technical language and to let people speak the plain truth from their hearts. Let them be able to answer this question: "What is our job and our work all about and why is it important to us and others?"

Ideally team visions should be devised by the team members. It should be revisited regularly because people and team's change. Vision must also be personal, otherwise it is merely a saying that everyone sort of agrees with.

Personal and team visions should also be short and to the point – a few sentences max! A word or two or short phrase if you can manage it. I often see team visions that state all kinds of wonderful truths about what they plan to focus on and accomplish, but they end up being another document in a drawer somewhere. If everyone on your team can't say it when asked, it is too complex and involved. If they can't say it with some kind of commitment and passion, it probably hasn't hit the right nerves. Difficultpeople.org is about "Understanding and Working with Difficult People." That is what we are passionate about.

Visions should have passion.

If they don't, who cares?

# 89. Conviction

Synonyms: sincerity; belief; passion

Antonyms: disbelief; doubt; skepticism

Passion and vision breed conviction.

Great leaders always seem to have a deep-rooted conviction in what they are about. I particularly like this tag, "what they are about." Conviction is not just a belief, it is a belief in what we are doing at any given point – what we are involved with and what we are working on.

One of the things that I have noted about people with conviction is how they bring it to whatever table they are at. When the vice-president of a major corporation takes over the CEO position of another business, his conviction and belief in himself and what he does is still there. It is not the corporation he works for, it is not the team he's on, it is not the people he works with. It is all of those and something more. It is who he is.

Dedication comes to mind as a term that might help to define conviction. Dedication to what one believes fundamentally and dedication to what one is focused on at this moment in time. Conviction is an attribute. It is not something that comes with a given job or territory. Great leaders bring it with them.

Conviction is one of those things that can rub off in many ways, too. People notice when you are dedicated. They notice when your heart and soul are into something. And they are much more likely to get on the 'A' train, when their leader is there showing the way.

**"It is not just a job – it is a personal commitment."**

(Peters and Austin)

If you don't care, you can't be committed and you won't have much conviction for what you are doing.

# 90. Courage

Synonyms: nerve; guts; bravery; audacity; daring

Antonyms: fear; fright; cowardice

> Courage is making (doing) things right,
>
> not just smoothing them over.
>
> (Maxwell, *The 21 IndispensibleQualities of Leadership*)

Got guts? Got chutzpah?

If you don't, you are in the wrong business. It takes guts to lead well. It takes a lot of chutzpah.

Wishy-washy doesn't cut it. Being a 'yes' person doesn't measure up. Obsequiousness is repulsive to a great leader.

Leaders stand up for themselves. They stand up for their teams. They stand up for what they believe is best.

This is one trait that I would think would be fairly obvious as a key to good leadership. Unfortunately it is the one characteristic that is far too often lacking.

> When I coach, courage is something I look for in my client, and then I look for it up and down the whole chain of command of their organization. Within a very short period of time I can name the people who really have it and those who don't.

**Leaders <u>don't</u> make excuses.**

**They <u>do</u> take responsibility.**

Leaders don't kowtow to the next up in the chain of command. They forward what they believe is right with openness and forthrightness.

Leaders don't back down from what they believe. They support and fight for their team.

Leaders may be afraid, but they use their fear to understand themselves and make intelligent choices.

Leaders don't just talk; they do. They make decisions and they make choices.

Courage isn't always easy. Choices can be very difficult. Leaders rely on the fundamentals of who they are and what they believe in when the going gets tough. They find the courage to make the decisions that they need to make. AND they always keep their people in mind throughout the process. Courage isn't about charging up over the hill without any regard for what is on the other side; it is about making intelligent choices that never lose sight of consideration for others.

**Be courageous for yourself.**

**Be courageous for others.**

Stand up and be counted as a leader.

That takes courage.

# 91. Fearless

Synonyms: brave; valiant;

Antonyms: fearful; apprehensive; scared

Are leaders fearless?

Well, if there are any, I haven't met them yet.

It is important for a leader to be courageous. It may not be good for anyone to be fearless. What is important at times is that they **appear** fearless.

Part of leadership is the responsibility of being the stable force for everyone to look up to during difficult situations. This is particularly true during significant change or crises situations. Being able to step back into a zone of self-control and show a calm, deliberate, intelligent demeanor in spite of your own inner angst is a valuable trait. Situations, and the people involved with/in them, take on a completely different aura when someone appears to be in control and in charge. It is much more likely that others will rally around the flag. Then the difficulties can be faced as a team, rather than everyone scattering in different directions.

Fear and upset are interesting phenomena. It is our feeling of lack of control that creates and exacerbates these negative feelings. Betty Perkins in her work "*Lion Taming*," suggests that all negative emotions are based in fear, which I feel is rooted in a sense of lack of control. When we complain, criticize, whine, and blame, we lack security, we lack self-confidence and self-worth, and we lack self-control. We also feel that we have no control of the situation or circumstances. These are all key leadership concepts we should be working on in ourselves.

When we have self-confidence, self-worth, and self-control, we are secure in who we are and what we are doing and have no need to give over our responsibility for our life to others by being 'in negativity.' So leadership really is fearless in the sense of ownership of our life and work.

It is not so much that leaders don't have moments and times when they feel anxious. Angst can help create the alertness and strength of purpose that are needed to face crises. Leaders use those feelings to jump start their momentum in order to deal with what is happening. Once they are in motion they reach a point where their determination and discipline kick in.

When we control our fear, we look inside ourselves for inner strength and we use that to make the best of the situation at hand. When our fear takes over, we tend to look outside ourselves for help, and we give over our control to what is happening. Worry is a good example of this type of fear and loss of control. We all worry, but when we worry to the point where it takes over our ability to function intelligently and constructively, we have given in to our fear in a sense. It is not that people like Winston Churchill and Abraham Lincoln didn't worry. They were strong leaders because they were capable of showing a strength in spite of the incredible difficulties they faced. They had an inner strength that helped lead their countries through major crises.

It takes no less a strength on a daily basis to deal with many of the things we all deal with every day. Want to know the potential great leaders? Look around and see those who are doing and not blaming. It is an interesting perspective!

# 92. Zany

Synonyms: crazy; madcap; wacky; screwball

Antonyms: sane; sensible; rational; reasonable


I am a goofball. My wife says it, my kids say it, and anyone who really knows me has seen it. It is not that I can't take things seriously, and I really do, sometimes. It is more that there is so much more enjoyment to be had in life when we can just let go and have some fun. Humor, a bit of craziness, the willingness to stick your neck out and look foolish are all ways that leaders can help people through the day to day operations at work and even, when used judiciously, through difficulties.

Granted not everyone can be zany or be a goofball. It is one of those traits that is better left to the experts unless you actually are that way naturally, but a good sense of humor is almost as good. Great leaders I quickly bring to mind weren't necessarily zany but many of them did have a good, if not subtle sense of humor.

More to the point is having the ability to be a bit lighter at times than someone who has a constant nose-to-the-grindstone, brook-no-nonsense, seriousness. Our work lives are difficult enough without having the ability and willingness to take a look at the lighter-side. Sometimes a leader's contribution to zaniness is simply allowing or even encouraging it in others.

Zany can be an attitude, an approach, or just some moments in time that are given over to less serious matters. There are usually at least one or two pretty 'crazy' people in a group. Give them a bit of leeway, especially during difficult times, to add that little extra to the team's workspace and work day.

It is also useful, every once in awhile, to just do something crazy yourself. Take a chance and see what it feels like. Yes, you might raise some eyebrows, but I guarantee that someone will have fun at your expense. There is nothing wrong with adding a bit of fun to the world. You do have to be willing to take yourself less seriously for that moment in time and you have to be willing to open yourself up to laughter and fun. It is useful to look at it from someone else's perspective and not from the idea that you are embarrassing yourself or that you will never be respected again. If anything, people respect even more those who are willing to stick their necks out and have a bit of fun.

Okay, I'll give you one example of goof-ball-ness: When I lived in Oklahoma there was a hill near our house that had a sign with "Dangerous Hill" written in big letters on it. One day when we were just starting up the hill in the family van I started screaming, "Aggghhhh, Oh no, It is going to get me," etc. My kids looked at me like I was crazy. Then I pointed out the sign. From that day on whenever anyone was in the car with us who hadn't been subjected to the 'dangerous hill,' we made a point of heading over that way. It didn't matter if it was my boss, a new recruit, or a friend.

Take a chance and have some fun with life. You will be the better for it and so will your team.


"Never work in a place where laughter is rare."

"Never work for a leader who doesn't laugh."

(Peters, *Re-imagine*)

# 93. Spontaneous

Synonyms: impulsive; spur-of-the-moment; unplanned; unstructured

Antonyms: structured; planned; prepared; well thought-out

Sometimes you just have to 'do it.' I have already talked about risk-taking and taking chances, but being spontaneous is both of those and something more. Great leaders are able to make decisions quickly, with limited information, when they need to. They can quickly, almost instantaneously, scan the possibilities and make the best possible choices without having to have meetings, weigh options, ask the boss, etc.

This is another trait that is often lacking in otherwise competent managers. They seem to have an underlying fear that unless they take considerable time and effort to make informed decisions that they will fail, appear to be 'not good enough' to their peers and bosses, and that any mistakes they might make will never be forgiven. If these types of worries are somehow the truth, then I would suggest it is time to look for another job anyway. I would hate to work under those kinds of pressures!

Yes, there are many times where making informed decisions is critical to success. But there are also times when we need to release ourselves from the necessity of controlling everything outside ourselves and be able to trust our instincts. Sometimes all the time we have to make a decision is seconds – if we take more time than that, we will lose out.

Being able and willing to make snap decisions is very important to good leadership. It is particularly important in a world where change is ongoing and the difference between having a multimillion dollar contract or your competitor getting it, might be that one-second decision you have to make in the board room when the person on the teleconference wants an answer. If you can't provide the key concession at that instant, they may simply turn the other way because of your indecisiveness, not necessarily because you weren't offering enough.

I also like to think of spontaneity from a more personal perspective. Being able to be spontaneous in your interactions with others allows a little more of an at ease relaxation to the work place. If everything is tightly controlled, including your demeanor, that is the overall feeling that will permeate your team and space. When we can relax and be more spontaneous personally, we add a measure of friendliness and kindliness to the mix. People who are more relaxed are typically more enervated and productive, not less.

If we are regular MBWAers (Peters, "Management by Walking Around"**), and we should be, spontaneity is essential. If everything is controlled and/or canned, you will never actually talk with people. You may talk at them, but you won't really get where you need to be because the whole process will be far too formal. [**See also my take on this, "**WLLF, Walk-Listen-Learn-Follow-up**," in *Managing Difficult Employees*, Chapter 6]


Relax, and be yourself. Have some fun with people, at work, and with your life.

# 94. Zesty*

Synonyms: spicy; stimulating; peppery

Antonyms: plain; mild


"Life is a great big canvas

and you should throw all the paint on it you can."

(Danny Kaye as quoted in *A Bend in the Road*, Lunden)


"Everything to excess! To enjoy the flavor of life, take big bites.

Moderation is for monks."

(Robert Heinlein)


Adding zest to life, especially life at work, makes sense. You have to be willing to see the value in it. Our work lives are dull enough (except for all those stresses). Your willingness to add that little bit extra can help energize and motivate people. Letting **them** add zest to their work is an even better tactic.

Zesty reminds me of the word 'spicy.' I like spicy things. I like being aware of and enjoying the spice of life. Opening up to the possibilities of a bit of extra spice in life is one of those little extras of leadership. It is not strictly necessary, but it sure can make a difference in the work place for you and for your team members.


Find your **"WOW!"**

(Tom Peters, see below)

No job, no relationship, no family, no interaction is perfect, unless...unless YOU make it that way, unless you see it. Open your eyes to the "WOWs" in your life.

EVERYthing potentially has a "WOW" factor present: Got a less than perfect job situation? There is a "WOW" there – discover it, breed it, make it happen, work for it. Create your own "WOW" and others will find their "WOW," too.

I can think of a dozen "WOWs" in my life without even working at it. **WOW!**

I can think of a dozen things about my work life that WOW me. **WOW!** [An even bigger WOW!)

Let your "WOWs" rule your day occasionally – always? You will be glad you did. At the very least spend a moment every day and add up your WOWs.

P.S. You CAN focus on other stuff, but it is not much FUN.

**Be a dispenser of enthusiasm!**

(Zander, conductor, from Peters, *The Circle of Innovation*)

*I first saw 'zesty' in Thomas Peters works. And while he doesn't own the word WOW, he has a whole book on it. It is well worth reading: *The Pursuit of WOW!*

# 95. Intensity

Synonyms: force; power; concentration; strength; vividness

Antonyms: weakness; impotence; powerlessness

There is a type of intensity to all good leaders. It might be the kind that is just below the surface and is a keenly focused fire of determination, or it could be a more outward, obvious intensity that motivates others and keeps the ball rolling through thick and thin.

Stick around a great leader long enough and you will not only sense it, but you will be affected by it. I think of it as a keenness of focus that never seems to get lost in spite of trying times, overwork, and shifting sands.

Take some time to really observe a person you feel has great leadership qualities. See how they approach things, the way they interact with others, their overall demeanor throughout a day, a week. If it isn't obvious right away, I think that eventually you will see that there is something within them that drives them onward. It is a personal commitment. Perhaps it is part determination, part commitment, part conviction, and a good bit of ownership. It also seems to be something more that is hard to put a finger on.

Fundamentally I think it has to do with personal integrity. Integrity in the sense of personal focus. It is what a person is all about. If it weren't for their ability to make this level of personal commitment in everything they tackle, they wouldn't do it.

Leaders have an intensity of personal commitment because it is who they are at the deepest level. They can't be anything else. They may not understand it about themselves. They may not even recognize it in themselves, but when they tackle something, it garners their complete dedication and determination. It is never half-hearted, or wishy-washy. It is jumping in with both legs, body, and head and getting completely wet right away.

I have seen this time and again in leaders that I admire. Perhaps another way to look at it is that they focus on what they are doing, not on themselves. When they worry, it is about doing things for others, getting things right, getting things done; it is never about how, why, and what "I look like." It is not about doing something for personal gain or for glory. It is about the work and what that means to them.

People who look outside themselves for acknowledgment and recognition as their motivation fail this aspect of leadership. They may seem intense, especially when they are upset and out-of-control, but they are not focused and committed.

Intensity in the sense of personal focus is what work means to us. The motivation comes from within and it starts with self-worth and self-control.

# 96. Charisma

Synonyms: charm; personality; magnetism

Antonyms: lackluster; uninspiring; bland; insipid; plain; character-less

There is something likeable about great leaders. It may not be the physical magnetism of a movie star or a model, but it is there. General Robert E. Lee was a quiet, unassuming, reserved man, but he had incredible charisma, and reportedly more than any other commander of his era, he could, just by his presence, motivate thousands and thousands of men to march into hell. Patton, on the other hand, had a very outgoing, almost bombastic, self-important personality. It was a charisma that was diametrically opposite of General Lee's, but it worked for him. He also led many men into the face of death.

I think that both these men, and many other great generals, presidents, world leaders, and others all had or have a charisma that comes from integrity. Whether they were overbearing and self-promotional or humble and reserved, these men and women were leaders by who they were as people.

We follow people who have true self-worth, self-confidence, and self-control. We quickly see through those who don't measure up in the sense of honor, trust, ownership, and responsibility. Patton (from the movie) is quoted as saying, "I know I am a prima donna. I admit it. The thing I don't like about Monty (English General Montgomery) is that he won't." [It should be understood that Patton and Montgomery rarely saw eye to eye and it is very possible Monty may have said the same type of thing about Patton.] Patton was ostentatious about his leadership and about himself, but he was also out there with his men. He had a charisma that led armies. They loved him for who he was.

Charisma is more about the perception of others than it is about how we personally pay attention to how we present ourselves to the rest of the world. Earlier in the book I wrote about how if we are consistently worrying, complaining, criticizing, and generally being negative, that is how others see us. By paying attention to ourselves we can turn that type of negativity around.

We may not be able to change our whole personality, but we can change others' perception of who we are by paying attention to specific things we do and say. An otherwise excellent leader may be shooting himself in the foot by being overcritical, because that is what shines through. Turn the criticism focus around and the rest of his personality has an opportunity to come through. People may then realize that in truth he is dedicated and sincere, hardworking and focused, and maybe even has a sense of humor.

Too often good, solid managers have very poor people skills for this very reason. Their inner self, their integrity and concern for others, is hidden beneath a lot of outward negativity, reaction to stress, angst, etc. I have seen this many times. Leaders who are at heart kind and hardworking come across as martinets and controllers because they don't pay attention to themselves and how others see them.

Let your true self shine through. That is what charisma really should be all about.

# 97. Showmanship

Synonyms: dramatic; theatrical; melodramatic

Antonyms: boring; dull; staid; tedious; demure

Showmanship is about being noticed. More importantly it is about having something that you care about noticed. It doesn't have to be ostentatious. Patton was a true showman. He liked being out there in view in all his regalia. He liked ceremony, awards, and honors. He felt it built esprit de corps. General Robert E. Lee was a showman, too, but it was in his bearing, his inner fervor, even in his reserved humility.

Sometimes it is good to have a bit of both if we are to be leaders. Showiness has its purposes. Pomp and circumstance, if judiciously used, are good for morale. There are times when a leader needs to put on a show. It might be simply to emphasize a point, or it could be about launching a new product line. The point is to gain everyone's attention in a positive way.

It certainly can be overdone. Too much showmanship and it loses its ability to affect people. Some people in leadership positions are so over-the-top in effusiveness that everyone wants to shy away, rather than pay attention.

Timing is just about everything when it comes to showmanship. Making just the right impact at the right time is a skill that good leaders learn. Too soon and people forget; too late and it has no oomph. I think leaders have to learn to be good actors, too – but they need to avoid 'faking it' and insincerity.

One should be able to put on a show when it is needed for morale,

Or

To make that one last burst of effort

Or

Be able to encourage people to hold on through one more reorganization

There is also a good bit of showmanship and acting skill in giving speeches and making presentations. Every field and business is slightly different in what is acceptable and reasonable in this light, but a little bit of extra pizzazz and energy can make a big difference in how what you are saying is being accepted (and whether half your audience is asleep or still in the room!).

It is also a very useful skill when you are working through difficult situations and with difficult people. I sometimes think of it as putting just the right emphasis on the right syl-la-ble. It can be that subtle AND that effective in its subtlety. Good acting isn't over-the-top unless you are doing melodramas or action adventures (I guess). It is often those tiny nuances in a smile, or a tear drop, that affect us the most.

Be dramatic when it counts; but never lose sight of being who you are. Otherwise people will see right through you.

# 98. Positivity*

Synonyms: upbeat; optimistic; enthusiastic

Antonyms: negativity; pessimism; cynicism

> Negativity breeds negativity
>
> Positivity breeds Positivity
>
> Choose wisely

This little gem has been a part of difficultpeople.org since I began writing all the books and other materials for the web site. I know that 'positivity' is not a 'real' word, or at least it wasn't before I coined it for difficultpeople.org (though I am told that scientists use it in another sense altogether).

I can't over-emphasize how much negativity and positivity matter in the work place. We have all seen it at work a thousand times. We have seen one or the other working a thousand times.

If there is a very negative (blaming, complaining, whining, worrying) person on a team it affects everyone. Just the same, I have seen upbeat and positive team members change the aura of a room or meeting in seconds.

What we don't see often enough,

**PAY ATTENTION because this is BIG**

Is how we are impacting others.

Our intensity can be seen as negativity if we don't pay attention. Our quality-mindedness can be seen as nit-picking if we don't pay attention to how we say things and how they are seen by others. Our 'get-it-done-ness' can be seen as 'in-your-face-pushiness' if we don't pay attention.

227

There are ALWAYS ways to say and do things that are more positive and less negative, including things such as negative evaluations. You have to be open and honest, and you have to watch how what you say and do impacts others, so you can respond quickly if you feel it has been taken the wrong way. This is something we can all work on throughout the rest of our lives. The goal is to get better. I doubt if there are many perfect people out there in this sense. Great leaders are sensitive to others and how what they do and say makes others feel. It is all about being kind.

Unfortunately we far too often focus on what is wrong with someone, and don't pay nearly enough attention to what is right or good about them. What we pay attention to is what people notice. It is also what we are reinforcing. Notice the greatness about someone (and I do believe that we all have greatness within us) and they will blossom.

I often stop myself for the briefest instant when I am interacting with others and ask this simple question, "Am I being kind?" And that quickly translates into, "Am I being as positive here as I can be?" When we try, we can be more positive and add more joy to the world.

### "Work is for Joy"

(Coachville, Graduate School of Coaching)

What a great perspective! This little gem hits us right where we live and work! How often can you describe your work as joy-filled?

I remember that when I was a university professor that if I left a lecture having had fun myself, I was not only energized, but I knew the students had some fun, too. I also knew they had learned more. If I left without that joy, I knew that lecture needed some improvement.

Find the joy in your work. It is there. You just need to make it that way, then focus on it. Be the positive catalyst you have the potential to be.

I wish you oodles and oodles of fun-filled work days.

# 99. Symbolizes

Synonyms: represents; signifies

Antonyms: misrepresent; feign

"Every minute is a symbolic opportunity...

You can choose to grasp it or squander it."

"Every system, seating arrangement, every visit is symbolic."

(Peters and Austin)

A leader represents his business, his broad organization, his team, his people, and himself. That is a great deal of responsibility. When we can keep this fact in mind as we do our work and as we interact with others, we can make the most of that opportunity. It also helps to remind us to pay attention to all those small details that can make a difference to our impact as a leader and as a person.

In this sense, every word we have discussed in this book makes a difference to the impact we have. As we build our strengths and work on our weaknesses, we are developing what we symbolize. These words, the ones we know that resonate with who we are and who we truly wish to be, are what we symbolize.

As you went through this book you were working on your truth, your image, by simply reading and thinking about all that this means to you. Every minute of every day we have opportunities to bring more of the truth about who we are as a leader to the surface. Every interaction we have with others is an opportunity to show and develop that truth.

Whether we want to admit it or not, leaders are symbols. And as such, it bears that we think about the responsibility we shoulder when we take up that mantle.

Consider the following:

> What am I symbolizing when I argue with another person?
>
> What am I symbolizing if I am less than open and forthright with someone.
>
> What am I saying if I am afraid to stand up for my team?
>
> What do others think when I blame my boss for all my problems?
>
> What is happening when I complain about my job, the facilities, my team, a team member?
>
> What do I symbolize when I spend all my time in meetings and in my office?

OR,

> What do I symbolize when I make an effort to be kind to everyone I interact with?
>
> How do people see me and what I represent when I keep them informed?
>
> How does someone else feel when I try to make them feel like they are the center of my focus for this time and space?
>
> What message do I send when I own my own life and all the decisions I make?
>
> How do I impact my work space when I focus on positivity instead of negativity?
>
> How do people feel when I make a concerted effort to listen, really listen to them?

These are decisions we make every day, many times every day, and many more, too. Each one sends a message. Each one is noticed by others.

Leadership is a big responsibility, even if you are only responsible for two other people.

Leadership is always a big responsibility.

**Lead wisely!**

# Appendix I

# Personal Leadership Commitment

The following scale is designed to assist you in a self-evaluation of your strengths and weaknesses as related to the qualities and values discussed at length in this book. We all have things we are really good at, and we have other things that we could do better and understand about ourselves more. Taking a careful look at 'where we stand' gives us the opportunity to know ourselves better, and provides us the information we need so we can focus on those things we feel we need to work on.

This is not an easy exercise to do. It takes a good bit of introspection and it takes making the effort to be completely honest with yourself about how you approach leadership (and life!). You may find that as you do this you will find it difficult, especially with certain values and qualities, to make a choice as to where you 'stand.' You can score this any way you like. One recommendation is to treat this like a sliding scale and if you feel a certain quality is a major strength of yours, place an 'X' on the left side of the 'Strengths' box; if you feel it is a strength, but could use a bit more focus and work, place an 'X' toward the right of the 'Strengths' box. If you feel it is a bit of a weakness, but you have done some work in that area and continue to improve, place an 'X' on the scale somewhere in the 'Need to Pay Attention' Box, and so on.

This exercise is for you and not for anyone else. I highly recommend keeping this personal information confidential and using it only for your own self-understanding and improvement.

If you are brave, you may want to ask a close friend or a close colleague who you feel you can trust to evaluate you honestly and fairly on how they perceive your leadership strengths related to this scale. Please make sure you are prepared to accept their perspective as to how they feel and let them know ahead of time that you sincerely appreciate their candor and what you will use the information for, i.e. self-improvement.

You can learn a great deal about yourself both through self-evaluation and through your willingness to ask your team members or peers. It can be an eye-opening experience. Balancing these perspectives can give you insight into what you really want to work on to improve your leadership ability.

We recommend copying these pages so that you can do this exercise several times.

You could also use this scale with your entire team IF you are prepared for the potential results and differences of perspective. Keep it as anonymous as possible and we highly recommend keeping it voluntary. The focus should always be to garner information about yourself for self-improvement purposes. Any other use is not recommended.


**Please Note**: This scale is NOT recommended for any type of formal evaluation process. It is not a standardized scale and has not been tested for validity or reliability, nor does it have any norms or data available. It is not meant to be scored and compared to other data.

| Value/Quality | Strengths | Good At | Need to Pay Attention To | Needs Work |
|---|---|---|---|---|
| 1. Integrity | | | | |
| 2. Honesty** | | | | |
| 3. Trust | | | | |
| 4. Ownership | | | | |
| 5. Accountable | | | | |
| 6. Responsibility | | | | |
| 7. Reliability | | | | |
| 8. Self-control** | | | | |
| 9. Loyalty | | | | |
| 10. Committed | | | | |
| 11.Conscientious | | | | |
| 12. Credible | | | | |
| 13. Stability | | | | |
| 14. Continuity | | | | |
| 15. Disciplined | | | | |
| 16. Humility | | | | |
| 17. Idealism | | | | |
| 18. Service | | | | |
| 19. Appreciation | | | | |

| | | | | |
|---|---|---|---|---|
| 20.Acknowledgment | | | | |
| 21. Respect | | | | |
| 22. Courteous | | | | |
| 23. Attention | | | | |
| 24. Support | | | | |
| 25. Grateful | | | | |
| 26. Recognition | | | | |
| 27. Celebration | | | | |
| 28. Ceremony | | | | |
| 29. Reward | | | | |
| 30. Caring | | | | |
| 31. Kindness** | | | | |
| 32. Empathy | | | | |
| 33. Compassion | | | | |
| 34. Patience | | | | |
| 35. Generous | | | | |
| 36. Responsiveness | | | | |
| 37. Grace | | | | |
| 38.Self-awareness** | | | | |
| 39. Awareness | | | | |
| 40. Visibility | | | | |
| 41. Connecting | | | | |

| | | | | |
|---|---|---|---|---|
| 42. Modeling | | | | |
| 43. Self-worth** | | | | |
| 44. Self-respect | | | | |
| 45.Self-confidence** | | | | |
| 46. Character | | | | |
| 47. Identity | | | | |
| 48. Quality | | | | |
| 49. Value-added | | | | |
| 50. Stretching | | | | |
| 51. Learning | | | | |
| 52. Education | | | | |
| 53. Renewal | | | | |
| 54. Solution-focused | | | | |
| 55. Catalyst | | | | |
| 56. Cultivate | | | | |
| 57. Rigorous | | | | |
| 58. Persistence | | | | |
| 59. Synthesizer | | | | |
| 60. Cohesion | | | | |
| 61. Attitude | | | | |
| 62. Consistent | | | | |
| 63. Cooperative | | | | |

| | | | | |
|---|---|---|---|---|
| 64. Competent | | | | |
| 65. Discerning | | | | |
| 66. Focus | | | | |
| 67. Organized | | | | |
| 68. Engagement | | | | |
| 69. Determined | | | | |
| 70. Energy | | | | |
| 71.Down-to-earth | | | | |
| 72. Simplicity | | | | |
| 73. Creativity | | | | |
| 74. Innovation | | | | |
| 75. Flexibility | | | | |
| 76. Experiment | | | | |
| 77. Risk-taking | | | | |
| 78. Fluidity | | | | |
| 79. Chances | | | | |
| 80. Imagination | | | | |
| 81. Friction-free | | | | |
| 82. Anticipates | | | | |
| 83. Facilitates | | | | |
| 84. Curiosity | | | | |
| 85. Initiative | | | | |

| | | | | |
|---|---|---|---|---|
| 86. Choices | | | | |
| 87. Passion | | | | |
| 88. Vision | | | | |
| 89. Conviction | | | | |
| 90. Courage | | | | |
| 91. Fearless | | | | |
| 92. Zany | | | | |
| 93. Spontaneous | | | | |
| 94. Zesty | | | | |
| 95. Intensity | | | | |
| 96. Charisma | | | | |
| 97. Showmanship | | | | |
| 98. Positivity** | | | | |
| 99. Symbolizes | | | | |

** Seven Keys to Understanding and Working with Difficult People

# Appendix II

# Values and Qualities

The following scale is designed to assist you in prioritizing those values and qualities discussed in this book that you feel will be most effective in your personal approach to leadership. This exercise can be helpful in gaining a perspective of what you feel is important for you as well as what qualities and values will be the best help for your employees and coworkers.

We recommend copying these pages so that you can do this exercise several times.

It may be useful and informative to do this the first time as a quick run-through exercise, in which you go with your gut feelings about the importance of these words to your own leadership style. Later, you may want to take more time, review the terminology and ideas presented in this book, and do the exercise again, trying to consider all the ramifications of each term for you and how it impacts other people you work with.

There is no scoring system; nor are there any right or wrong answers. This is simply designed to gain insight into how we as individuals approach our work and life. Coupled with the scale in Appendix I this will provide you valuable information on what you value and who you want to be as a leader.

Keep in mind that you will probably relate very strongly to some of these values and qualities while others may not 'work for you.' Feel free to add terms that you feel strongly about in your own leadership style. This list represents the terms I felt gave me the best venue for discussing the qualities that make a great leader. You may find other similar terms or variations on these terms work better for you or you may have other words that represent more strongly how you view leadership. There is no right or wrong list. Go with what works for you.

I like to keep things simple, so one approach to this scale is to pick your top ten values and qualities and make them into your personal priority list.

A useful exercise is to pick your top 25, then narrow that down further, and further, until you have identified the top 3 to 5 most important qualities you feel represent great leadership. It can give you further insight into who you are and what you feel is most important about how you approach your work: then you can focus on making sure you are living those values.

| Value/Quality | Top Priority | Important | Good to Think About | Not my Cup of Tea |
|---|---|---|---|---|
| Integrity | | | | |
| Honesty** | | | | |
| Trust | | | | |
| Ownership | | | | |
| Accountable | | | | |
| Responsibility | | | | |
| Reliability | | | | |
| Self-control** | | | | |
| Loyalty | | | | |
| Committed | | | | |
| Conscientious | | | | |
| Credible | | | | |
| Stability | | | | |
| Continuity | | | | |
| Disciplined | | | | |
| Humility | | | | |
| Idealism | | | | |
| Service | | | | |
| Appreciation | | | | |

| | | | | |
|---|---|---|---|---|
| Acknowledgment | | | | |
| Respect | | | | |
| Courteous | | | | |
| Attention | | | | |
| Support | | | | |
| Grateful | | | | |
| Recognition | | | | |
| Celebration | | | | |
| Ceremony | | | | |
| Reward | | | | |
| Caring | | | | |
| Kindness** | | | | |
| Empathy | | | | |
| Compassion | | | | |
| Patience | | | | |
| Generous | | | | |
| Responsiveness | | | | |
| Grace | | | | |
| Self-awareness** | | | | |
| Awareness | | | | |
| Visibility | | | | |

| | | | | |
|---|---|---|---|---|
| Connecting | | | | |
| Modeling | | | | |
| Self-worth** | | | | |
| Self-respect | | | | |
| Self-confidence** | | | | |
| Character | | | | |
| Identity | | | | |
| Quality | | | | |
| Value-added | | | | |
| Stretching | | | | |
| Learning | | | | |
| Education | | | | |
| Renewal | | | | |
| Solution-focused | | | | |
| Catalyst | | | | |
| Cultivate | | | | |
| Rigorous | | | | |
| Persistence | | | | |
| Synthesizer | | | | |
| Cohesion | | | | |
| Attitude | | | | |

| | | | | |
|---|---|---|---|---|
| Consistent | | | | |
| Cooperative | | | | |
| Competent | | | | |
| Discerning | | | | |
| Focus | | | | |
| Organized | | | | |
| Engagement | | | | |
| Determined | | | | |
| Energy | | | | |
| Down-to-earth | | | | |
| Simplicity | | | | |
| Creativity | | | | |
| Innovation | | | | |
| Flexibility | | | | |
| Experiment | | | | |
| Risk-taking | | | | |
| Fluidity | | | | |
| Chances | | | | |
| Imagination | | | | |
| Friction-free | | | | |
| Anticipates | | | | |
| Facilitates | | | | |

| | | | | |
|---|---|---|---|---|
| Curiosity | | | | |
| Initiative | | | | |
| Choices | | | | |
| Passion | | | | |
| Vision | | | | |
| Conviction | | | | |
| Courage | | | | |
| Fearless | | | | |
| Zany | | | | |
| Spontaneous | | | | |
| Zesty | | | | |
| Intensity | | | | |
| Charisma | | | | |
| Showmanship | | | | |
| Positivity** | | | | |
| Symbolizes | | | | |

** Seven Keys to Understanding and Working with Difficult People

# CHOICES

*I am going to worry all the time and kick myself*
*whenever I do something*
*that is remotely stupid.*

*I am going to feel bad whenever anyone puts me*
*down, be depressed because no one likes me,*
*and get frustrated all the time*
*because no one listens to me.*

*I am not going to take care of myself when I get*
*tired, over-worked, or ill*
*or take time for myself because I have way too*
*much to do.*

*I am going to accept everything bad that anyone*
*says about me,*
*because it is all true.*

*I am going to wallow in self-pity.*
*Or*

*I am going to stop worrying and look at the
brighter side of life.*

*I am going to pay attention to my thoughts
and feelings and when I start to think negatively
or to kick myself,
I am going to turn my thoughts around and say
supportive, kind things to myself.*

*I am going to be self-confident, believe in myself,
and maintain a calm, cool, collected persona
wherever I am and with whomever I am with.*

*I am going to be assertive, kind, and compassionate
in all my dealings with others.*

*I am going to pay attention to my communications
and always try to present
a positive me to the rest of the world.*

*I am going to believe in myself.*

difficultpeople.org

# Appendix IV

# Annotated Bibliography

Works by Dr. Joseph Koob

## Books with a Business Focus
## Business Trilogy: Dealing with Change

### Difficult Situations - Dealing with Change

Difficult situations can certainly produce a great deal of angst and as a result, difficult people. From my own long personal experience, I know that when things are tough, I can get much more difficult than normal. Those are the times when I know I need to deal with my own stuff.

### Honoring Work and Life: 99 Words for Leaders to Live By

This book provides a foundation of key ideas that focus on Leadership (and Personal) qualities, attributes, and behaviors that honor not only our work but our life. It is my firm belief that true leaders work to serve their fellow employees, their team, their company, their customers, as well as their families and friends. This is about understanding and working on those attributes that make great leaders.

### Leaders Managing Change

Leaders Managing Change is about understanding and dealing with the ongoing stresses of constant change in the business world today, but most importantly it is about leadership. When I thought about the concerns that are a regular part of high turnover rates, leadership changes, acquisitions and mergers, and the myriad of other transitions businesses face today, the focus came down to leadership. Good leaders get things done. This book focuses on knowledgeable leadership, i.e. what you need to know to help you deal with change as a leader. It presumes you are already inspired, good, intelligent, and practical. This book is about making a difference.

Dr. Joseph Koob

# Business Trilogy: Succeeding at Work

## Dealing with Difficult Coworkers

This work is one that based on my research is a needed addition to the difficult people literature. There are a number of books available that discuss difficult people in the workplace, but do not focus specifically on coworkers. There are different dynamics between bosses and employees, employees and their peers, and employees with their bosses. The emphasis here is on  helping people solve the difficulties they have at work with someone who is relatively speaking a 'coworker,' or 'colleague,' in other words, someone whose 'rank' or 'job' is roughly on the same level as theirs.

## Succeeding with Difficult Bosses

Have a tough boss? This is a practical, in-the-trenches approach to succeeding with a difficult authority figure. So much of our appreciation and success at work seems to have to do with who our boss is – as a manager (good or bad), as a leader (one who inspires or does not), and, most importantly, as a person (does he/she care). What we do care the most about in a person who is above us in the chain of command is their willingness (or not) to acknowledge, appreciate, and recognize who we are and the effort we put forth.

## Managing Difficult Employees

This book is first and foremost about leadership. What can I do as a manager and leader to create a work environment that fosters positive personnel development? In other words, preventive maintenance – avoiding difficult people concerns and difficult situations through competent management and inspired leadership. It is also about the knowledge you need, and the skills you can learn to be able to deal with people concerns that are present or that may arise?

*Honoring Work and Life*

## Dealing with Difficult Customers

(for Employees, Companies, and Customer Service Personnel)

This book is all about putting the gamut of customer relations and interactions into a perspective that is workable, livable, and supports you, the customer contact person, throughout.

While many businesses do provide extensive customer relations training, the focus is often fairly one way – aimed at keeping business. We present you with extensive insight and knowledge about the customer's perspective, what you need to know as a company representative to fulfill your job, the internal and external support you need, and the tools and skills to communicate effectively with difficult customers.

## Caring for Difficult Patients: A Guide for Nursing Professionals

I believe that the Nursing profession is one of the most admired in America. We think of Nurses as professional: that is, they have a knowledge base and skill set that is unique and valued – the quality of their work is important to them; and we think of Nurses as people who care about their patients – they are concerned with our well-being when we are under their care. These considerations are the focal point for discussing how to best deal with difficult patients.

# Books with a Personal Focus

## Understanding and Working with Difficult People

We believe this book presents the most comprehensive material available about being successful with difficult people. This book is designed to be a practical, accessible introduction to the very broad topic of dealing with difficult people/difficult behaviors. Since every difficult situation is different, the focus here will be on building a basic understanding of how you interact with difficult people, what makes difficult people tick, and the most fundamental skills you can bring to the table to help change these encounters for the better.

## ME! A Difficult Person?

This is second of our signature books. This book focuses on learning more about yourself. Most of us are occasionally difficult or seen as difficult by others. This may simply be a matter of different perspectives, or it may mean that we have some inner work to do. This book is concerned with understanding more about how you come across to others, and understanding more about who you are as a person. It is also concerned with self-improvement – making changes that will help make your interactions with others significantly better, and that will bring you more peace, comfort, and joy in your life.

## Dealing with Difficult Strangers

Being successful in difficult situations with strangers is all about what you can bring to the situation. You will find a tremendous amount of useful information and skills included in this book that can make a significant difference in how you approach difficult strangers, how you feel as a result of these difficult encounters, and how you can emerge without a negative experience having ruined your day.

**Difficult Spouses? Improving and Saving Your Relationship with Your Significant Other**

Are you having difficulties in your current relationship? Facing a divorce? Newly divorced and trying to understand what happened and what you could have done about it? We feel this book has value not only for couples who are simply having difficulties in their relationships with their significant others; those facing divorce, recently divorced couples; and for people entering new relationships. The focus is on developing the knowledge, skills, and tools to help your relationship be successful.

**Succeeding with Difficult Professors (and Tough Courses)**

A course for college students at all levels. What you need to know to make the most of your college career. This course has two main sections: "Getting along with Difficult Professors," and "Succeeding in Tough Classes." The first section will discuss ideas and skills you can use to get through personal difficulties with professors. The second section will focus on techniques, study skills, and approaches that will help you get the grades you want.

**Guiding Children**

Guiding and working with children is on the mind of every parent. This book focuses on skills and tools to help you as a parent provide the best possible environment for your child's development by avoiding difficulties through intelligent upbringing. This book is not only about helping you to guide your children through concerns that arise, but it is even more about enjoying your children. They do grow up, much faster than we expect. Take advantage of the tremendous joy they can bring into your life and the vast understanding of life that they provide. You will be glad you did.

**A Perfect Day: Guide for a Better Life**

Dr. Koob's award-winning book about working toward your own personal perfect day. Best Book Non-fiction, 1999, Oklahoma Writer's Federation; Merit award 2000, Writer's Digest.

# Bibliography

## Books and other works on Change and Leadership

Bolles, Richard N., *What Color is Your Parachute?* Ten Speed Press, Berkeley, CA, 1987.

Bridges, William, *Managing Transitions: Making the Most of Change*, Perseus Books, Cambridge, 1991.

Bridges, William, *Transitions: Making Sense of Life's Changes*, Perseus Books, Cambridge, 1980.

Buckingham, Marcus, & Coffman, Curt, *First, Break All the Rules: What the World's Greatest Managers Do Differently*, Simon and Schuster, New York, 1999.

Collins, J., and Porras, J., *Built to Last: Successful Habits of Visionary Companies*, Harper Business, NY, 2001.

Collins, Jim, *Good TO Great: Why Some Companies Make the Leap...and Others Don't*, Harper Business, NY, 2001.

Cooper, Robert and Sawaf, Ayman, *Executive EQ: Emotional Intelligence in Leadership & Organizations*, Grisset/Putnam, New York, 1996.

Crane, Thomas, *The Heart of Coaching*, FTA Press, San Diego, 1998.

Deits, Bob, Life *After Loss: A Personal Guide Dealing with Death, Divorce, Job Change and Relocation*, Fisher Books, Tucson, 1988.

Dominhguez, Linda R., *How to Shine at Work*, McGraw Hill, 2003.

Drucker, Peter F., *Managing in a Time of Great Change*, Truman Talley Books, NY, 1995.

Evard, Beth L. And Gipple, Craig A., *Managing Business Change for Dummies*, Hungry Minds, Inc., NY, 2001.

Farson, Richard and Keyes, Ralph, *Whoever Makes the Most Mistakes Wins: The Paradox of Innovation*, Free Press, NY, 2002.

Fortgang, Laura Berman, *Take Yourself to the Top: The Secrets of America's #1 Career Coach*, Warner Books, New York, 1998.

Gates, Bill, *Business @ the Speed of Thought: Succeeding in the Digital Economy*, Warner Books, New York, 1999.

Gerstner, Jr., Louis, V, *Who Says Elephants Can't Dance? Leading a Great Enterprise Through Dramatic Change*, Harper-Business, New York, 2002.

*Going Through Bereavement–When a loved one dies*, Langeland Memorial Chapel, Kalamazoo, MI.

Grieve, Bradly T., *The Blue Day Book: A Lesson in Cheering Yourself Up*, Andrews McMeel Publishing, Kansas City, 2000.

Goldratt, Eliyahu M., *Critical Chain*, North River Press, Great Barrington, MA, 1997.

Hammer, Michael and Champy, James, *Reengineering the Corporation: A Manifesto for Business Revolution, HarperBusiness*, New York, 1993.

Hoffer, Eric, *The Ordeal of Change*, Harper & Row, NY, 1952.

Jeffreys, J. Shep. *Coping with Workplace Change: Dealing with Loss and Grief*, Crisp Productions, Menlo Park, CA, 1995.

Johnson, Spencer, *Who Moved My Cheese*, G. P. Putnam, New York, 1998.

Kanter, Rosabeth Moss, *The Change Masters: Innovation & Entrepreneurship in the American Corporation*, Simon & Schuster, New York, 1983.

Kelley, Robert, *How to be a Star at Work: Nine Breakthrough Strategies You Need to Succeed*, Random House, New York, 1998.

Koob, Joseph E. II, *Difficult Situations: Dealing with Change*, NEJS Publications, Saline, MI, 2004.

Kotter, John P, *Leading Change*, Harvard Business School Press, Boston, 1996.

Kotter, John P, *The Leadership Factor*, Free Press, New York, 1988.

Kouzes, J. and Posner, B., *Credibility: How Leaders Gain and Lose it; Why People Demand it*, Jossey-Bass Publishers, San Francisco, 1993.

Kuster, Elizabeth, *Exorcising Your Ex*, Fireside, New York, 1996.

Leonard, George, *Mastery: The Keys to Success and Long-term Fulfillment*, Plume, NY 1992.

Lunden, Joan, and Cagan, Andrea, *A Bend in the Road is Not the End of the Road,* William Morrow, New York, 1998.

Maxwell, John C., *The 21 Indispensible Qualities of Leadership: Becoming the Person Others Will Want to Follow*, Thomas Nelson Publishers, Nashville, 1999.

Maxwell, John C., *The 17 Indisputable Laws of Teamwork: Embrace them and Empower Your Team*, Thomas Nelson Publishers, Nashville, 2001.

Maxwell, John C., *21 Irrefutable Laws of Leadership*, Thomas Nelson, Inc., Nashville, 1998.

Milwid, Beth, *Working With Men: Professional Women Talk About Power, Sexuality, and Ethics*, Beyond Words, Kingsport, TN, 1990.

McKay, Harvey, *Swim with the Sharks: Without Being Eaten Alive*, William Morrow Co., New York, 1988.

Messer, Bonnie J., *Dealing with Change*, Abington Press, 1996.

Montalbo, Thomas, *The Power of Eloquence: Magic Key to Success in Public Speaking*, Prentive-Hall, Englewood Cliffs, N.J., 1984.

Pasternack, Bruce and Viscio, Albert, *The Centerless Corporation: A New Model for Transforming Your Organization for Growth and Prosperity*, Fireside, New York, 1998.

Peters, Tom, *The Circle of Innovation: You Can't Shrink Your Way to Greatnness*, Vintage Books, New York, 1999.

Peters, Tom, *Liberation Management: Necessary Disorganization for the Nanosecond Nineties*, Faucett Columbine, New York, 1992.

Peters, Tom, and Waterman, Robert, *In Search of Excellence: Lessons from America's Best-Run Companies*, Harper & Row, New York, 1982.

Peters, Tom, and Austin, Nancy, *A Passion for Excellence: The Leadership Difference*, Random House, New York, 1985.

Peters, Tom, *The Pursuit of WOW! Every Person's Guide to Topsy-Turvy Times*, Vintage Books, New York, 1994.

Peters, Tom, *Professional Service Firm 50: Fifty Ways to Transform Your "Department" into a Professional Service Firm whose Trademarks are Passion and Excellence*, Alfred A. Knopf, 1999.

Peters, Tom, *Re-imagine! Business Excellence in a Disruptive Age*, DK, London, 2003.

Peters, Tom, *Thriving on Chaos: Handbook for a Management Revolution*, Alfred Knopf, New York, 1987

Popcorn, Faith, *EVEolutuon: The Eight Truths of Marketing to Women*, Hyperion Books, 2001.

Smith, Hyrum W. The *10 Natural Laws of Successful Time and Life Management: Proven Strategies for Increased Productivity and Inner Peace*, Warner Books, New York, 1994.

Talbot, Kay, *The Ten Biggest Myths About Grief*, Abbey Press, St. Meinrad, IN, 2000.

Waterman, Robert H., Jr., *The Renewal Factor: How The Best Get And Keep The Competitive Edge*, Bantam, New York, 1986.

Whitmore, John, *Coaching for Performance*, Nicholas Brealey Publishing, London, 1999.

# Difficult People Materials

Axelrod, A and Holtje, J., *201 Ways to Deal with Difficult People*, McGraw-Hill, New York, 1997.

Bell, A. and Smith, D., *Winning with Difficult People*, Barron's, New York, 1997

Bramson, Robert M., *Coping with Difficult Bosses*, Fireside, New York, 1992.

Bramson, Robert M., *Coping with Difficult People*, Anchor Press, New York, 1981.

Braunstein, Barbara, *How to Deal with Difficult People*, Skillpath Publications, Mission, KS, 1994. [Tapes]

Brinkman, R. and Kirschner, R., *Dealing with People You Can't Stand*, McGraw-Hill, New York, 1994.

Carter, Jay, *Nasty Bosses: How to STOP BEING HURT by them without stooping to THEIR level*, McGraw-Hill, New York, 2004.

Case, Gary and Rhoades-Baum, *How to Handle Difficult Customers*, Help Deck Institute, Colorado Springs, 1994.

Cava, Roberta, *Dealing with Difficult People: How to Deal with Nasty Customers, Demanding Bosses and Annoying Co-workers*, Firefly Books, Buffalo, NY, 2004.

Cava, Roberta, *difficult people: How to Deal with Impossible clients, Bosses, and Employees*, Firefly Books, Buffalo, NY, 1990.

Cavaiola, A. And Lavender, N., *Toxic Coworkers: How to Deal with Dysfunctional People on the Job*, New Harbinger Publications, Oakland, CA, 2000.

Costello, Andrew, *How to Deal with Difficult People*, Ligori Publications, Liguri, MI, 1980.

Crowe, Sandra, *Since Strangling Isn't An Option*, Perigee, New York, 1999.

Diehm, William, *How to Get Along with Difficult People*, Broadman Press, Nashville, 1992.

Felder, Leonard, *Does Someone Treat You Badly? How to Handle Brutal Bosses, Crazy Coworkers...and Anyone Else Who Drives You Nuts*, Berkley Books, NY, 1993.

First, Michael, Ed., *Diagnostic and Statistical Manual for Mental Disorders*, 4th Edition, American Psychiatric Asso.,Washington, 1994.

Friedman, Paul, *How to Deal with Difficult People*, SkillPath Publications, Mission, KS, 1994.

Gill, Lucy, *How to Work with Just About Anyone*, Fireside, New York, 1999.

Griswold, Bob, *Coping with Difficult and Negative People and Personal Magnetism*, Effective Learning Systems, Inc., Edina, MN. [Tape]

Holloway, Andy, "Bad Boss Blues," *Canadian Business*, 24 Oct 2004.

Hoover, John, *How to Work for an Idiot: Survive & Thrive Without Killing Your Boss*, Career Press, Princeton, NJ, 2004.

Jones, Katina, *Succeeding with Difficult People*, Longmeadow Press, Stamford, CT, 1992.

Keating, Charles, *Dealing with Difficult People*, Paulist Press, New York, 1984.

Littauer, Florence, *How to Get Along with Difficult People*, Harvest House, Eugene, 1984.

Lloyd, Ken, *Jerks at Work: How to Deal with People Problems and Problem People*, Career Press, Franklin Lakes, NJ, 1999

Lundin, W. and Lundin, J., *When Smart People Work for Dumb Bosses: How to Survive in a Crazy and Dysfunctional Workplace*, McGraw-Hill, New York, 1998.

Markham, Ursula, *How to deal with Difficult people*, Thorsons, London, 1993.

Meier, Paul, *Don't Let Jerks Get the Best of You: Advice for Dealing with Difficult People*, Thomas Nelson, Nashville, 1993.

Namie, G. and Namie, R., *the Bully at Work*, Sourcebooks, Inc., Naperville, IL, 2000.

Osbourne, Christina, *Dealing with Difficult People*, DK, London, 2002.

Oxman, Murray, *The How to Easily Handle Difficult People, Success Without Stress*, Morro Bay, CA, 1997.

Perkins, Betty, *Lion Taming: The Courage to Deal with Difficult People Including Yourself*, Tzedakah Publications, Scramento, 1995.

Rosen, Mark, *Thank You for Being Such A Pain: Spiritual Guidance for Dealing with Difficult People*, Three Rivers Press, New York, 1998.

Segal, Judith, *Getting Them to See It Your Way: Dealing with Difficult and Challenging People*, Lowell House, Los Angeles, 2000.

Solomon, Muriel, *Working with Difficult People*, Prentice Hall, Englewood Cliffs,1990.

Toropov, Brandon, *The Complete Idiot's Guide to Getting Along with Difficult People*, Alpha Books, New York, 1997.

Toropov, Brandon, *Manager's Guide to Dealing with Difficult People*, Prentice Hall, Paramus, NJ, 1997.

Turecki, Stanley, *The Difficult Child*, Bantam Books, NY, 1989.

Weiner, David L., *Power Freaks: Dealing with Them in the Workplace or Anywhere*, Prometheus Books, Amherst, New York, 2002

Weiss, Donald, *How to Deal with Difficult People*, Amacon, New York, 1987.

Dr. Joseph Koob

# Recommended Readings

Dewey, John, *Democracy and Education*, Norwood Press, Norwood, MA, 1916.

Dewey, John, *Education and Experience*, Kappa Delta Pi Publications, Macmillian, New York, 1938.

Dyer, Wayne, *Pulling Your Own Stri*ngs, Funk and Wagnalls, New York, 1978.

Dyer, Wayne, *Your Erroneous Zones*, Funk and Wagnalls, New York, 1976.

Dyer, Wayne, *Your Sacred Self*, Harper, New York, 1995.

Guraik, David B., Editor, *Webster's New World Dictionary*, World Publishing, New York, 1972.

Heinlein, Robert, *Time Enough for Love*, New English Library, New York, 1974.

Hesse, Hermann, *Narcissus and Goldmund*, Bantam, New York, 1971.

James, M, and Jongeward, D. *Born to Win*, Addison-Wesley, 1971.

Koob, Joseph, *A Perfect Day: Guide for A Better Life*, NEJS Publications, Lawton, OK, 1998.

Parrott, Thomas Marc, Ed., *Shakespeare: Twenty-three Plays and the Sonnets*, Charles Scribner's Sons, Washington, D.C., 1938.

Pirsig, Robert, *Zen and the Art of Motorcycle Maintenance*, Bantam, New York, 1980.

Rand, Ayn, *Atlas Shrugged*, Signet Books, New York, 1957.

Redman, Ben Ray, Editor, *The Portable Voltaire*, Viking Press, New York, 1949.